'Thomas Ogden, whose inspiring and prolific work deepens and widens the very heart of psychoanalysis, makes a new and refreshingly clear proposal in his new book. The distinction between an epistemological psychoanalysis and an ontological psychoanalysis has been evolving and crystallizing since Winnicott's paradigm-changing writings. This superb collection of essays, with moving and vivid clinical vignettes alongside an evocative, scholarly appreciation of the founding psychoanalytic authors Freud and Klein, exemplifies the meaning of an ontological psychoanalytic practice *par excellence*. The analyst whose focus lies in the evolution of the Self, for both analyst and analysand, will not only love this book but also feel immensely grateful to Ogden for offering, once again, his breath-taking insights and generative reflections on living and being in the analysing situation and beyond.'

Jan Abram, *author of* The Surviving Object:
Psychoanalytic clinical essays on psychic *survival-of-the-object*

'In his latest thought-provoking book, Thomas Ogden explores our ways of being, expressing ourselves, and finding vitalization in life. His writing is fluid and subtle, capable of capturing and shaping the most genuine human experience of living and feeling, that is, of coming into existence. His book is not only that of a psychoanalyst at the height of his creativity, but also of one of the great humanist intellectuals at work today.'

Elias M. da Rocha Barros, *supervising and training analyst, Brazilian Psychoanalytic Society, São Paulo, and Fellow of the Institute of Psychoanalysis, London*

'In this stunning extension of his prior contributions, Ogden opens fresh insight into central questions of life—what it means to be a person in a world of others. My experience while reading felt like that when I first read Freud: I felt myself with a Virgil who explained, as we visited confusing experiences I had had from across my life, clinical and personal. I found this work so useful and such a pleasure to read that I read it twice, not only to milk the learning, but also for the sheer pleasure I find when I hear the voice of so gifted a writer.'

Warren S. Poland, *author of* Intimacy and Separateness in Psychoanalysis

Coming to Life in the Consulting Room

Ogden sets out a movement in contemporary psychoanalysis toward a new sensibility, reflecting a shift in emphasis from what he calls "epistemological psychoanalysis" (having to do with knowing and understanding) to "ontological psychoanalysis" (having to do with being and becoming).

Ogden clinically illustrates his way of dreaming the analytic session and of inventing psychoanalysis with each patient. Using the works of Winnicott and Bion, he finds a turn in the analytic conception of mind from conceiving of it as a thing—a "mental apparatus"—to viewing mind as a living process located in the very act of experiencing. Ogden closes the volume with discussions of being and becoming that occur in reading the poetry of Robert Frost and Emily Dickinson, and in the practice of analytic writing.

This book will be of great interest not only to psychoanalysts and psychotherapists interested in the shift in analytic theory and practice Ogden describes, but also to those interested in ideas concerning the way the mind and human experiencing are created.

Thomas H. Ogden, MD, is the author of 12 books of essays on the theory and practice of psychoanalysis, most recently *Reclaiming Unlived Life*; *Creative Readings: Essays on Seminal Analytic Works*; and *Rediscovering Psychoanalysis*. He was awarded the 2012 Sigourney Award for his contribution to psychoanalysis.

THE NEW LIBRARY OF PSYCHOANALYSIS
General Editor: Alessandra Lemma

The New Library of Psychoanalysis was launched in 1987 in association with the Institute of Psychoanalysis, London. It took over from the International Psychoanalytical Library which published many of the early translations of the works of Freud and the writings of most of the leading British and Continental psychoanalysts.

The purpose of the New Library of Psychoanalysis is to facilitate a greater and more widespread appreciation of psychoanalysis and to provide a forum for increasing mutual understanding between psychoanalysts and those working in other disciplines such as the social sciences, medicine, philosophy, history, linguistics, literature and the arts. It aims to represent different trends both in British psychoanalysis and in psychoanalysis generally. The New Library of Psychoanalysis is well placed to make available to the English-speaking world psychoanalytic writings from other European countries and to increase the interchange of ideas between British and American psychoanalysts. Through the *Teaching Series*, the New Library of Psychoanalysis now also publishes books that provide comprehensive, yet accessible, overviews of selected subject areas aimed at those studying psychoanalysis and related fields such as the social sciences, philosophy, literature and the arts.

The Institute, together with the British Psychoanalytical Society, runs a low-fee psychoanalytic clinic, organizes lectures and scientific events concerned with psychoanalysis and publishes the *International Journal of Psychoanalysis*. It runs a training course in psychoanalysis which leads to membership of the International Psychoanalytical Association – the body which preserves internationally agreed standards of training, of professional entry, and of professional ethics and practice for psychoanalysis as initiated and developed by Sigmund Freud. Distinguished members of the Institute have included Michael Balint, Wilfred Bion, Ronald Fairbairn, Anna Freud, Ernest Jones, Melanie Klein, John Rickman and Donald Winnicott.

Previous general editors have included David Tuckett, who played a very active role in the establishment of the New Library. He was followed as general editor by Elizabeth Bott Spillius, who was in turn followed by Susan Budd and then by Dana Birksted-Breen. Current members of the Advisory Board include Giovanna Di Ceglie, Liz Allison, Anne Patterson, Josh Cohen and Daniel Pick.

Previous members of the Advisory Board include Christopher Bollas, Ronald Britton, Catalina Bronstein, Donald Campbell, Rosemary Davies, Sara Flanders, Stephen Grosz, John Keene, Eglé Laufer, Alessandra Lemma, Juliet Mitchell, Michael Parsons, Rosine Jozef Perelberg, Richard Rusbridger, Mary Target and David Taylor.

A full list of all the titles in the New Library of Psychoanalysis main series is available at https://www.routledge.com/The-New-Library-of-Psychoanalysis/book-series/SE0239

For titles in the New Library of Psychoanalysis 'Teaching' and 'Beyond the Couch' subseries, please visit the Routledge website.

Coming to Life in the Consulting Room

Toward a New Analytic Sensibility

Thomas H. Ogden

Routledge
Taylor & Francis Group

LONDON AND NEW YORK

Cover image: © Sandra Ogden

First published 2022
by Routledge
4 Park Square, Milton Park, Abingdon, Oxon OX14 4RN

and by Routledge
605 Third Avenue, New York, NY 10158

Routledge is an imprint of the Taylor & Francis Group, an informa business

British Library Cataloguing-in-Publication Data
A catalogue record for this book is available from the British Library

Library of Congress Cataloging-in-Publication Data
Names: Ogden, Thomas H., author.
Title: Coming to life in the consulting room: toward a new analytic
sensibility / Thomas H. Ogden.
Description: Abingdon, Oxon; New York, NY: Routledge, 2022. | Series:
The
new library of psychoanalysis | Includes bibliographical references and
index. |
Identifiers: LCCN 2021029304 (print) | LCCN 2021029305 (ebook) | ISBN
9781032132655 (hardback) | ISBN 9781032132648 (paperback) | ISBN
9781003228462 (ebook)
Subjects: LCSH: Psychoanalysis. | Psychotherapy. | Psychoanalysts. |
Psychotherapists. | Psychotherapist and patient.
Classification: LCC RC504 .O33 2022 (print) | LCC RC504 (ebook) | DDC
616.89/17--dc23
LC record available at https://lccn.loc.gov/2021029304
LC ebook record available at https://lccn.loc.gov/2021029305

ISBN: 978-1-032-13265-5 (hbk)
ISBN: 978-1-032-13264-8 (pbk)
ISBN: 978-1-003-22846-2 (ebk)

DOI: 10.4324/9781003228462

Typeset in Bembo
By Deanta Global Publishing Services, Chennai, India

Also by Thomas H. Ogden

Non-Fiction

Projective Identification and Psychotherapeutic Technique
The Matrix of the Mind: Object Relations and the Psychoanalytic Dialogue
The Primitive Edge of Experience
Subjects of Analysis
Reverie and Interpretation: Sensing Something Human
Conversations at the Frontier of Dreaming
This Art of Psychoanalysis: Dreaming Undreamt Dreams and Interrupted Cries
Rediscovering Psychoanalysis: Thinking and Dreaming, Learning and Forgetting
On Not Being Able to Dream: Selected Essays, 1994-2005 (available only in Hebrew)
Creative Readings: Essays on Seminal Analytic Works
The Analyst's Ear and the Critic's Eye: Rethinking Psychoanalysis and Literature (co-authored with Benjamin Ogden)
Reclaiming Unlived Life: Experiences in Psychoanalysis

Fiction

The Parts Left Out: A Novel
The Hands of Gravity and Chance: A Novel
This Will Do . . . : A Novel

For Glen Gabbard, Michael Kilchenstein, and John Schneider

Contents

Acknowledgments

I would like to thank *The Psychoanalytic Quarterly* for use of the following papers in this volume:

"Ontological Psychoanalysis or 'What Do You Want to Be When You Grow Up?'" *Psychoanalytic Quarterly* 88:661-684, 2019. © *The Psychoanalytic Quarterly.*

"How I Talk with My Patients," *Psychoanalytic Quarterly* 87:399–414, 2018. © *The Psychoanalytic Quarterly.*

"Dreaming the Analytic Session: A Clinical Essay," *Psychoanalytic Quarterly* 86:1–20, 2017. © *Psychoanalytic Quarterly.*

"Toward a Revised Form of Analytic Thinking and Practice: The Evolution of Analytic Theory of Mind," *Psychoanalytic Quarterly* 89:219–243, 2020. © *Psychoanalytic Quarterly.*

"On Language and Truth in Psychoanalysis," *Psychoanalytic Quarterly* 85:411–426, 2016. © *Psychoanalytic Quarterly.*

The International Journal of Psychoanalysis has kindly granted permission to use the following papers in this volume:

"The Feeling of Real: On Winnicott's 'Communicating and Not Communicating Leading to a Study of Certain Opposites,'" *International Journal of Psychoanalysis* 99:1288–1304, 2018. © The Institute of Psychoanalysis.

"Destruction Reconceived: On Winnicott's 'The Use of an Object and Relating Through Identifications,'" *International Journal of Psychoanalysis* 97:1243–1256, 2016. © The Institute of Psychoanalysis.

I would like to thank *Psychoanalytic Perspectives* for permission to use the following paper in this volume: "Experiencing the Poetry of Robert Frost and Emily Dickinson," *Psychoanalytic Perspectives* 17:183–188, 2020. © *Psychoanalytic Perspectives.*

I am grateful to *The Journal of the American Psychoanalytic Association* for permission to use the following paper in this volume: "Analytic Writing as a Form of Fiction," *Journal of the American Psychoanalytic Association* 69, 2021. © *The Journal of the American Psychoanalytic Association*.

I would like to thank Henry Holt and Company for permission to use Robert Frost's "Stopping by Woods on a Snowy Evening."

I would like to express my appreciation of the valuable contributions that Gina Atkinson and Patricia Marra have made to the production of this book.

This book would be quite a different book without the thoughtful editing done by my wife, Sandra Ogden.

Preface

This book, taken as a whole, describes a movement currently emergent in psychoanalysis toward a new and generative analytic sensibility—toward new qualities of receptivity and responsiveness to what is occurring in the analytic session. This sensibility facilitates states of mind in which patient and analyst more fully come to life in the analytic process. This new sensibility is reflected in the interplay of two inseparable dimensions of analytic thinking and practice. One of these dimensions, which I call *epistemological psychoanalysis* (having to do with knowing and understanding) was introduced and developed by Freud and Klein; the other, *ontological psychoanalysis* (having to do with being and becoming), was pioneered and elaborated by Winnicott and Bion (Introduction and Chapter 1). Winnicott's and Bion's shifts of emphasis from the epistemological to the ontological represent a revolutionary change in psychoanalytic theory and practice. The goal of ontological psychoanalysis is that of facilitating the patient's *experience of creatively discovering for himself, of being and becoming more fully alive, more fully himself.*

I offer my own "creative readings" (Chapters 2 and 4) of two of Winnicott's seminal papers—"Communicating and not communicating leading to a study of certain opposites" (1963) and "The use of an object and relating through identifications" (1967)—both of which are concerned with the ways in which experience comes to be endowed with "all the sense of real" (1963, p. 184). These papers, while having been written more than 50 years ago, are of key importance to the movement in psychoanalysis with which I am concerned in this volume.

Two chapters (Chapters 3 and 5) are devoted to the way I practice psychoanalysis. Here I attempt to provide the reader a sense of what I mean when I say we must invent psychoanalysis for each patient.

I find that I naturally speak differently with each analysand, as we naturally speak differently with our mother or father or brother or sister or close friend. Paradoxically, it takes a good deal of analytic experience to be able to speak naturally. When I talk with a patient, I am present with the patient in the act of *experiencing with her* aspects of her life that she has not yet been able to live. In talking with a patient, I *describe* what I sense is occurring and do little *explaining.* I see my "off-ness" in a session not as a failure, but as an opportunity. I view analysis as a co-creation of patient and analyst at an unconscious level in which reverie—waking dreaming—is an indispensable element. My reveries are some of the most alive, most real, most surprising, most growth-promoting, most difficult, and most painful parts of the session.

The chapters that follow (Chapters 6 and 7) explore two developments in analytic theory: the change in the analytic conception of the birth of the mind and the role of language usage in intuiting what is occurring in the session.

With regard to an analytic theory of mind (Chapter 6), I see a critical turn in analytic thinking as one moves from the conception of mind developed by Freud, Klein, and Fairbairn—who see mind as "an apparatus for thinking"—to that developed by Winnicott and Bion, who see mind as *a living process* located in the very act of experiencing.

Concerning the role of language usage, the "shape" of the analytic dialogue—its continuities and discontinuities, its tangents and non sequiturs—constitutes a medium in which patient and analyst communicate what cannot be said in any other way (Chapter 7).

I close this book by inviting the reader to join me in meandering in spheres in which dreaming and experiencing, being and becoming, hold center stage. In this spirit, I first take up the experience of reading the poetry of Robert Frost and Emily Dickinson (Chapter 8), and then turn to the experience of analytic writing (Chapter 9).

References

Winnicott, D. W. (1963). Communicating and not communicating leading to a study of certain opposites. In *The Maturational Processes and the Facilitating Environment.* New York: International Universities Press, 1965, pp. 179–192.

Winnicott, D. W. (1967). The use of an object and relating through identifications. In *Playing and Reality.* New York: Basic Books, 1972, pp. 86–94.

INTRODUCTION

Notes on being and becoming

The question "What do you want to be when you grow up?" lies at the heart of what I shall be discussing in this book. This question masquerades as an inquiry concerning occupational goals, but in fact it is a question concerning the most fundamental aspects of one's states of being and becoming: "Who (what kind of person) do you want to be *now, at this moment*, and what kind of person do you aspire to become?"

"Growing up" requires force of will in concert with unconscious psychic work that can be achieved only with the help of parents who facilitate psychic development. The need to grow up constitutes an intense, unrelenting force within us that leads us to hurl ourselves against the walls of internal and external constraints in our effort to achieve increasing depth and breadth of who we are and who we might become. Those internal constraints, the limits of our present personality, against which we do battle, are many and various. It is difficult to let go of our belief in our parents' powers to magically protect us and in our own magical power to achieve idealized versions of ourselves. It is disturbing to recognize that, despite ourselves, we tenaciously hold to what we feel to be destructive aspects of ourselves, of our internal and external parents, and of our social system and culture. Growing up, becoming more fully ourselves, requires that we not simply loosen our hold on identifications with both healthy and pathological aspects of our parents, we must "kill something vital in them—not all in one blow and not in all respects, but contributing to their dying" (Loewald, 1979, p. 395).

DOI: 10.4324/9781003228462-101

As we throw ourselves against these external and internal constraints, we find ourselves experiencing not only feelings of fear and insecurity, but also feelings of exhilaration as we revise (at times, overthrow) the mores, values, fears, and ambitions of our parents as well as the ways they had of expressing themselves. We experience feelings of joy and a sense of satisfaction and triumph in shedding the role and identity of a child and claiming our place as an adult member of the *present* generation, a generation with its own views and understandings of what is of value, its own art forms never before conceivable (for example, in music, dance, literature, science), its conception of fairness, equality, democracy, and every other system of morality, and even the qualities of emotion that can be experienced.

All of this, this full range of feeling and thought—the anguish and self-doubt as well as the joy and sense of triumph—is integral to, and inextricable from, what is entailed in the violence of growing up.

In considering the question, "Who do you want to be when you grow up?" the word *want* is limited by the circumstances into which one is born, which are at once inevitable and a matter of chance. For example, it is in a sense inevitable that we, as the products of the interplay of the genetics of our parents, are members of the family into which we are born and are influenced by the cultural roots and practices of that family; and at the same time, from another perspective, it is utterly a matter of chance that we are the children of the parents we were dealt (parents who more or less fortuitously met and created a human embryo). The sense of inevitability, when we become able to consider the circumstances of our lives, also applies to the economic and social situation into which we are born. From this perspective, chance, in all of its forms, plays a powerful role in determining the limits of the sort of person whom we might be able to imagine, much less be able to "want" (aspire) to become. Some children and adults are able to transcend, to a very large degree, the limits of their parents' personalities and the social, cultural, economic, and political circumstances into which they are born. This is not to say that they shed their identity and adopt a new one, for to do so is equivalent to becoming someone else, to obliterating one's existence. Rather, what I have in mind is that while we are never free of the reality of external circumstances, neither are we entirely slaves of circumstance.

A patient with whom I have worked in analysis comes to mind in connection with the complexity of the question, "What [who] do you want to be when you grow up?" He was an only child born into a family in which his parents were emotionally absent, consumed by the battle they were waging against one another. The patient told me in the first session, "I raised myself." From very early on in the analysis, Mr. M accused me unrelentingly of not being of any value to him: he was "getting nothing out of the analysis." He had a habit of continuing his rants as he left the office, taking his time as he departed, often extending his session by a minute or two or three. This went on for more than a year.

I regularly imagined telling this patient that he was free to find an analyst who could help him. But over time I came to like and respect Mr. M, and began to view his insistence that he was making no progress in the analysis as a wish that the analysis would never end (because it never began, in his fantasy). He was refusing (in his words) "to be cheated out of a real analysis." I took his feeling of being cheated by me to be an unconscious expression of his insistence that he not be, once again, robbed of his childhood. Some years into the analysis when his disparagement of me and the analysis had become stale, even to him, I said, "I think that your refusal to leave here before you've received what is rightfully yours—a real analysis, a full session—is the healthiest part of you." Mr. M asked if I was making fun of him. I said, "I've never been more serious." As we talked about his rage at me, including his admission that he sometimes enjoyed being rageful, he stopped extending our sessions in the way that he had (a fact neither of us mentioned).

Later in our work together, Mr. M not infrequently talked about the early years of the analysis. At one point he said, he had been "childish." I replied, "I see it differently. I'd say you were being a child when that was who you needed to be."

Mr. M, I believe, discerned that he could not genuinely grow up without experiencing a form of childhood in the relationship with me (though he would not have formulated the situation in these terms). It has been my experience in working with patients that it is impossible to "skip" (do without) a phase of development; no living creature—plant or animal—can do so. Mr. M could "raise himself" *in appearance only.* I believe that the impossibility of "skipping" a phase of development (in Mr. M's case, doing without a childhood lived with emotionally sensitive and responsive parents) applies to every phase of psychic development: not having lived a given phase of development radically distorts or renders impossible subsequent experiences of growing up.

To my mind, symptom formation is a means by which patients put on hold the problem of growing up, of coming more fully into being. Individuals for whom symptoms serve this function—which includes all of us to different degrees—are at a loss regarding what it means to take the next steps in growing up, for they have had insufficient experience with a caretaking person engaged with them in ways of being that are more evolved than their own. From this perspective, patients hold firmly to their symptoms, their closed loops of thinking and behaving, because they do not know what else to do.

It seems to me misleading to view a patient's tenacious hold on his symptoms as deriving primarily from the narcissistic gratification involved in drawing attention to himself or herself (demeaningly referred to as "secondary gain"); nor is he or she "resisting" the analyst's efforts to conduct the analysis; nor trying "to kill the analysis and the analyst"; nor entering into "psychic retreats" to insulate himself or herself from what is happening in the transference. Rather, I view patients' symptoms as critically important markers of "where the bodies are buried," that is, where in the psyche and soma certain aspects of the patient's sense of who she is and who she might become have been exiled and perhaps have died (see Ogden and Gabbard, 2010 and Chapter 6 for further discussion of symptom formation).

In dealing with the aspects of self that have been buried alive, it is of the utmost importance for the analyst to respect the patient's defenses. To directly or indirectly undermine defenses—including those involved in the patient's symptomatology—is to obscure or demean, or send further into exile, the markers, the "places" in the personality where a battle to come into being is silently being waged. The voices of the "bodies that have been buried alive and remain alive" are not only violently angry and frightened, they are also plaintive. When all goes well enough in an analysis, the patient, late in the analysis, may be able to feel profound sadness in response to realizing that, even with the analyst's help, not all of the buried bodies, who had once held the potential to become alive and real aspects of the patient's personality, can be reclaimed, reincorporated (or incorporated for the first time) into the patient's sense of who she is and who she is becoming.

4

The "experience of being buried alive" that I am referring to here is not to be equated with repression or dissociation, both of which are based on conceptions of psychic disturbance that have to do with stripping thoughts and feelings of the quality of conscious awareness and the quality of psychic integration, respectively. By contrast, the experience I am referring to involves loss of the sense of aliveness and "the feeling of real" (Winnicott, 1963, p. 184) as a human process continually in the making, as opposed to a conception of mental illness as a division of the mind "horizontally" in the case of repression, and "vertically" in the case of dissociation.

In the extreme, a patient may not even have "dead bodies" to unearth and bring to life again because they were never born alive in the first place, they were stillborn. This outcome is usually the result of severe abuse and neglect in infancy and childhood. A patient, Ms. J, cried as she told me in our initial meeting, "I've tried therapy and analysis a number of times, and each time either the therapist or I finally gave up because nothing was happening." After she told me about her parents' unrelenting, insanely vicious attacks on her throughout her life, beginning in her infancy, I said, "You couldn't tell your previous therapists, and they couldn't see, or if they did, they couldn't tell you, that you died in childhood." Sobbing, she said, "That's right, but it's hopeless, isn't it? What can I do if I'm already dead?" I said, "You put your question in the form, 'What can *I* do?' There hasn't been a 'we' in any sentence you've uttered today. I don't think you really know what the word means."

Ms. J said, "I don't know what anything or anyone means. I'm completely lost all the time. Even when I'm by myself looking for my car in a parking lot or on the street, I can't find it. I have no sense of direction. I have no memory with which to orient myself." This was the beginning of a long analysis in which the patient was able very gradually to become someone whom she recognized and experienced as herself. This occurred first in relation to me. "Becoming," for Ms. J, included the extremely painful recognition that she had died, or perhaps more accurately, she had never lived as a child, and the life of that child could not be reclaimed. But that did not mean that she could not create new life in the course of our work together, a life in which she slowly, incrementally became able to experience with people other than me.

I feel honored when a patient who has died psychically (and often has a life-threatening physical illness such as lupus, a lymphoma, or a seizure disorder) entrusts me with his or her internal dead or stillborn bodies, whose deaths need to be respectfully witnessed (Poland, 2000) and mourned before new growth can occur in a place tended by the two of us.

And the quiet word *when*, in the question, "What (who) do you want to be when you grow up?" plays an important role in the process of growing up, or refusing to settle for growing up *in form only*, or feeling frightened of growing up, or feeling unable to grow up. We all live in that sliver of time between *then*, referring to the past, and *then*, referring to the future, and we must sense the moment *when* the time is right for us to grow up in particular ways. I use the word "sense," as opposed to "determine" or "decide," because a maturational advance is an experience that feels as if it has a mind and a will of its own. That "mind and will" is usually on key, but it is fallible, and when it falters, the help of other people is critical, for it takes at least two people to think beyond a certain point (Bion, 1962; Ogden, 2010). Thinking, for all of us, takes place within the limits of our personality, and on our own, we cannot think in a way that transcends those limits.

"Growing up" is hard-won at every stage of life, but in adulthood, advances in becoming more fully oneself become less easily measured than in earlier periods of life. In infancy, childhood, and adolescence, "progress" may be to some degree gauged by such landmarks as learning to walk and talk, adjusting to nursery school and kindergarten, graduating from high school and college or some other schooling, and so on. As an adult, achieving greater maturity—being and becoming more the person one is and might become—is primarily an internal matter. One is increasingly on one's own in sensing change, for instance, in becoming able to be more fully present in one's thoughts, emotions, and bodily sensations; to be a more loving, more compassionate, more generous parent or grandparent, or more deeply, personally engaged in one's marriage or one's work; to be actively in the process of developing one's unique creative potentials and discovering forms in which to give them shape; or to be more fully engaged in putting into practice a more humane system of values and ethical standards; and so on. Promotions, awards, and publications are notoriously unreliable measures of growing up, but the sense of emptiness and meaninglessness that often accompanies such events may be helpful in laying bare the ways in which one is finding it difficult to become the person one once had thought one might become.

A patient comes to mind in this regard. By the time he was in his mid–50s, Mr. K had been awarded the highest honors in his field. He began analysis because of a feeling of depression he had lived with for as long as he could remember. He was a very "good patient," thoughtful and self-reflective, punctual, and replete with perceptive comments on occurrences in his own life and events in the larger world. Nonetheless, the analysis felt emotionally flat to me.

Mr. K called halfway through one of his early morning sessions to tell me that he had overslept and would not be coming to his session. The following day he began by apologizing for not "having the common courtesy to show up" for his session—a bit excessive in his repentance, I thought. I quite spontaneously said, "I thought it was a good session yesterday. I read the newspaper. Of course, with you in mind."

The patient laughed deeply, a belly laugh in which I joined him. We both were enjoying the multiple levels of meaning that were alive in the interaction. Mr. K and I took pleasure in my irreverent response that mirrored his disguised defiance as well as my indicating that the session took place regardless of where the patient happened to be when it occurred. Mr. K was beginning to come into his own, to feel free to experience and express in his own way a wider range of feeling states, and to laugh at himself when I spoke to him with a note of irony. As is always the case, it was necessary for me to be free to be myself as an analyst if the patient was to be free to become more fully himself. It is here that prescribed analytic technique often interferes with creating a generative analytic process.

From the perspective I am developing in this book, psychopathology in general might be viewed as the inability to grow, to come more fully into being in a way that feels real. The experience of not growing, not changing, not becoming, is a state of being in which one is unable to dream, to engage in unconscious psychological work, and consequently unable to dream oneself up, to "dream oneself into existence" (Ogden, 2004, p. 858). To put this in still other words, a significant measure of the severity of psychic illness is the degree to which becoming (growing up) has ceased.

The experience of "being" and "becoming," in health, is a fundamental quality of being alive from the very beginning to the very end of life. Winnicott wrote in his personal diary (not read by anyone until after his death), "Oh God! May I be alive when I die" (Winnicott, 2016, p. 298). Here Winnicott was expressing his wish to become more fully himself in his experience of dying.

References

Bion, W. R. (1962). *Learning from Experience*. London: Tavistock.

Loewald, H. (1979). The waning of the Oedipus complex. In *Papers on Psychoanalysis*. New Haven, CT: Yale University Press, 1980, pp. 384–404.

Ogden, T. H. (2004). This art of psychoanalysis: Dreaming undreamt dreams and interrupted cries. *The International Journal of Psychoanalysis*, 85:857–877.

Ogden, T. H. (2010). On three types of thinking: Magical thinking, dream thinking, and transformative thinking. *The Psychoanalytic Quarterly*, 79: 314–347.

Ogden, T. H. & Gabbard, G. O. (2010). The lure of the symptom. *Journal of the American Psychoanalytic Association*, 58:533–544.

Poland, W. (2000). The analyst's witnessing and otherness. *Journal of the American Psychoanalytic Association*, 78:17–34.

Winnicott, C. (2016). D. W. W.: A reflection. In *The Collected Works of Donald Winnicott, Vol. 12, Appendices and Bibliographies*. Oxford, UK: Oxford University Press, p. 298.

Winnicott, D. W. (1963). Communicating and not communicating leading to a study of certain opposites. In *The Maturational Processes and the Facilitating Environment*. New York: International Universities Press, 1965, pp. 179–192.

1

ONTOLOGICAL PSYCHOANALYSIS OR "WHAT DO YOU WANT TO BE WHEN YOU GROW UP?"

A friend who was stationed in London as a U.S. Army psychiatrist during the Second World War regularly attended Winnicott's rounds on the Adolescent Unit of Paddington Green Hospital. He told me that Winnicott asked every adolescent he saw the question "What do you want to be when you grow up?" and placed great weight on his or her response (Ira Carson, personal communication, 1983). This question is perhaps the most important question any of us asks ourselves from very early in life until the moment just before we die. Who would we like to become? What kind of person do we want to be? In what ways are we not ourselves? What is it that prevents us from being more the person we would like to be? How do we become more of the person we feel we have the potential to be and the responsibility to be? These are the questions that bring most patients to therapy or analysis, though they are rarely aware that this is the case, being more focused on finding symptomatic relief. At times, the goal of treatment is to bring a patient from a state of not being able to form such questions to a state in which he is.

Having begun by focusing on the second half of the title of this chapter, I will now turn to the first half—"ontological psychoanalysis"—while trying all the while to hold in mind the question, "What do you want to be when you grow up?"

DOI: 10.4324/9781003228462-1

Epistemological and ontological psychoanalysis

A radical change has occurred, rather unobtrusively, in the theory and practice of psychoanalysis in the course of the past 70 years, a change for which, until recently, I have not had a name. That transformation involves a shift in emphasis from *epistemological* (pertaining to knowing and understanding) psychoanalysis to *ontological* (pertaining to being and becoming) psychoanalysis. I view Freud and Klein as the founders of a form of psychoanalysis that is epistemological in nature, and I consider Winnicott and Bion as the principal contributors to the development of ontological psychoanalysis. Finding words to describe this movement in psychoanalysis holds a good deal of personal significance for me. This chapter is, in a sense, an account of the movement in my own thinking from a focus on unconscious internal object relationships to a focus on the struggle in which each of us is engaged to more fully come into being as a person whose experience feels real and alive to himself or herself.

Though it is beyond the scope of this chapter to review the work of the many analytic thinkers who have contributed to the development of the ontological aspect of psychoanalysis, I will refer the reader to the work of a few of those authors: Balint (1992), Berman (2001), Civitarese (2010, 2016), Eshel (2004), Ferro (2011), Gabbard (2009), Greenberg (2016), Grinberg (1980), Grotstein (2000), Laing (1960), Levine (2016), Milner (1950), Searles (1986), Semrad (Semrad and Day, 1966), Stern et al. (1998), Sullivan (1962), Will (1968), and Williams (2019).

It is important for the reader to bear in mind throughout this chapter that *there is no such thing as ontological psychoanalysis or epistemological psychoanalysis in pure form.* They coexist in mutually enriching relationship with one another. They are ways of thinking and being—sensibilities, not "schools" of analytic thought or sets of analytic principles or analytic techniques. So there is much in the work of Freud and Klein that is ontological in nature, and much in the work of Winnicott and Bion that is epistemological.

Epistemological psychoanalysis, as I am using the term, refers to a process of gaining knowledge, arriving at understandings of the patient, particularly understandings of the patient's unconscious inner world and its relation to the external world. These understandings serve to organize one's experience in a way that is of value in addressing one's emotional problems and achieving psychic change.

10

The analyst's interpretations are meant to convey understandings of the patient's unconscious fantasies, wishes, fears, impulses, conflicts, aspirations, and so on. As Laplanche and Pontalis (1973) put it,

> Interpretation is at the heart of the Freudian doctrine and technique. Psychoanalysis itself might be defined in terms of it, as the bringing out of the latent meaning.
>
> (p. 227)

They continue:

> Interpretation reveals the modes of the defensive conflict and its ultimate aim is to identify the wish that is expressed by every product of the unconscious.
>
> (p. 227)

From a similar perspective, Klein (1955) describes her work with a child in analysis:

> The child expressed his phantasies and anxiety mainly in play, and I consistently interpreted its meaning to him … I was also guided throughout by two other tenets of psycho–analysis established by Freud, which I have from the beginning regarded as fundamental: that the exploration of the unconscious is the main task of psycho–analytic procedure and that the analysis of the transference is the means of achieving this aim.
>
> (p. 123)

The most important clinical intervention, from an *epistemological* vantage point, is the interpretation of the transference: the analyst conveys in words to the patient his or her understanding of the ways in which the patient is experiencing the analyst as if he or she were a real or imagined figure from the patient's infancy or childhood. "In the transference, infantile prototypes re-emerge and are experienced with a strong sensation of immediacy" (Laplanche and Pontalis, 1973, p. 445). Experiencing the present as if it were the past blocks psychic change: it constitutes a closed loop that repeats itself endlessly, allowing little or no room for new possibilities to develop.

By contrast, I am using the term *ontological psychoanalysis* to refer to a dimension of psychoanalysis in which the analyst's primary focus

11

is on facilitating the patient's efforts to become more fully himself. Winnicott (1971a) concisely describes the difference in perspective between ontological and epistemological psychoanalysis:

> I suggest that in her writings Klein (1932), in so far as she was concerned with play, was concerned almost entirely with the use of play [as a form of symbolization of the child's inner world] ... This is not a criticism of Melanie Klein or of others who have described the use of the child's play in the psycho-analysis of children. It is simply a comment on the possibility that ... the psychoanalyst has been too busy using play content to look at the playing child, and to write about playing as a thing in itself. It is obvious that I am making a significant distinction between the meanings of the noun "play" and the verbal noun "playing."
>
> (pp. 39–40)

Winnicott is making a distinction here between the *symbolic meaning* of "play" and the *state of being* involved in "playing." Arriving at understandings of the symbolic meaning of play is the domain of epistemological psychoanalysis; working in and with the state of being involved in playing is the domain of ontological psychoanalysis.

From an ontological perspective,

> *Psychotherapy takes place in the overlap of two areas of playing, that of the patient and that of the therapist. The corollary to this is that where playing is not possible then the work done by the therapist is directed towards bringing the patient from a state of not being able to play into a state of being able to play.*
>
> (Winnicott, 1971a, p. 38, original emphasis)

The analyst's role, as described in this passage (and in Winnicott's work as a whole) is quite different from the role of the analyst in the analysis of a predominantly epistemological sort. While in episte-mological psychoanalysis the analyst's role centrally involves con-veying in the form of interpretation the analyst's understanding of the leading edge of anxiety in the present moment of the analysis, in a predominantly ontological psychoanalysis the analyst had better "wait" (Winnicott, 1969, p. 86) before conveying his or her under-standings to the patient:

> It appalls me to think how much deep change I have prevented or delayed … by my personal need to interpret. If only we can wait, the patient arrives at understanding creatively and with immense joy, and I now enjoy this joy more than I used to enjoy the sense of having been clever.
>
> (Winnicott, 1969, p. 86)

From the perspective of ontological psychoanalysis, it is not the knowledge arrived at by patient and analyst that is the central point; rather, it is the patient's experience of "arriv[ing] at understanding creatively and with immense joy," an experience in which the patient is engaged not predominantly in searching for self-understanding, but in *experiencing* the process of becoming more fully himself.

Winnicott (1971b), in one of his late papers, "Dreaming, fantasy-ing, and living," reaches a conclusion that lies at the heart of his opus and differentiates his approach from Klein's, in particular, and epis-temological psychoanalysis in general. For Winnicott, unconscious fantasy is a vicious cycle that entraps one in one's inner world. In describing a portion of an analysis, he writes,

> For me the work of this session had produced an important result. It had taught me that fantasying interferes with action and with life in the real or external world, but much more so it interferes with dream[ing] and with the personal or inner psy-chic reality, the living core of the individual personality.
>
> (1971b, p. 31)

Winnicott (1971c), almost in passing, in his "transitional object" paper, uses a phrase that I view as the process underlying successful psychoanalysis and every other form of psychic growth: we "weave other-than-me objects into the personal pattern" (p. 3). In other words, we take something that is not yet part of us (for example, an experience with a spouse or a friend or in reading a poem or listening to a piece of music) and weave it into who we are in a way that makes us more than who we were before we had that expe-rience, before weaving the experience into our personal pattern.

Winnicott, here, in developing the ontological aspect of psycho-analysis, is inventing language as he goes—"to weave other-than-me objects into the personal pattern"—a way of speaking about psychic growth that I have never come across anywhere else.

When the patient or analyst is unable to engage in playing, the analyst's attention must be directed to this problem, for it precludes the patient and analyst from *experiencing* "the overlap of two areas of playing." If the analyst is unable to engage in playing, he must determine whether his inability to engage in this state of being (playing is not simply a state of mind, it is a state of being) is a reflection of what is occurring between him and the patient (possibly a profound identification with the patient's lifelessness) or a reflection of his own inability to genuinely engage in playing, which would likely require that he return to analysis.

It might be argued that what I am calling epistemological psychoanalysis and ontological psychoanalysis are merely different ways of looking at a single analytic endeavor. There are, indeed, vast areas of overlap of the two. For instance, the analyst may offer a sensitively worded, and well-timed, interpretation of the patient's fear that only one of the two of them—the patient or the analyst—can be a man at any given time because if both are men at the same time, they will inevitably enter into a battle to the death of one of them. The outcome of such an understanding may not simply be enhanced self-knowledge on the part of the patient, but as importantly, a greater sense of freedom to be himself as a grown man.

It is not difficult to find ontological thinking in the work of Freud and Klein. Take, for instance, Freud's (1923) idea that the analyst attempts

> to avoid so far as possible reflection and the construction of conscious expectations, [and attempts] not to try to fix anything he heard particularly in his memory, and by these means to catch the drift of the patient's unconscious with his own unconscious.
>
> (p. 239)

"He [the analyst] should simply listen, and not bother about whether he is keeping anything in mind" (Freud, 1912, p. 112). "Simply listen[ing]" is a state of being, a way of being with the patient.

Also representative of Freud's ontological thinking is his famous statement, "*Wo Es war, soll Ich werden*": "Where id [it] was, there ego [I] shall be" (Freud, 1933, p. 80). What had been experienced as other to oneself ("the it") is incorporated into one's being (who I am, who I "shall *be*," who I am becoming). (Freud [1926] was explicit in his instructions "to keep [psychoanalytic concepts] in contact with the popular mode of thinking" [p. 195]. Thus, *Das Ich* is better translated as "the I" and *Das Es* as "the it.")

Notwithstanding the overlap and interplay of the epistemological and ontological dimensions of psychoanalysis, and the fact that neither ever exists in pure form, it seems to me that there are a great many experiences that occur in the course of an analysis that are predominantly epistemological or predominantly ontological in nature. To my mind, these two aspects of psychoanalysis involve quite different modes of therapeutic action. Therapeutic action characterizing the epistemological dimension of psychoanalysis involves arriving at understandings of previously unconscious thoughts, feelings, and bodily experience, which help the patient achieve psychic change. By contrast, therapeutic action characterizing ontological psychoanalysis involves providing an interpersonal context in which forms of experiencing, states of being, come to life in the analytic relationship that were previously unimaginable by the patient (for instance, the states of being involved in *experiencing* transitional objects and phenomena (Winnicott, 1971c) and in *experiencing* the silent communication at the core of the self (Winnicott, 1963).

It is beyond the scope of this chapter to compare what I am calling the ontological dimension of psychoanalysis and the rather diverse set of ideas grouped under the general heading "existential psychoanalysis." Much of existential psychoanalysis is concerned with conscious awareness, intentionality, freedom, and responsibility, which are seen as inextricably linked (which undercuts the Freudian concepts of unconscious pressures and limitations of freedom). Major contributors to existential psychoanalysis include Ludwig Binswanger, Victor Frankl, Rollo May, Otto Rank, Jean-Paul Sartre. Neither will I take up the philosophical underpinnings of ontology and epistemology. I am restricting myself to a general linkage of the former with being and becoming, and the latter with gaining knowledge and understanding.

15

Being alive, feeling all the sense of real

I will now attempt to state in more detail what I have in mind when I refer to the practice of ontological psychoanalysis. I will focus first on the work of Winnicott, and later on that of Bion.

Winnicott, in almost every paper he wrote, introduces and describes states of being not previously recognized in the analytic literature, for instance, the state of "going on being" (Winnicott, 1949, p. 245), a phrase that is all verb (verbal noun) and devoid of a subject, thus capturing something of a very early subjectless state of being; the state of being involved in the mother surviving while being destroyed by the infant (Winnicott, 1969); and the state of being involved in "primary maternal preoccupation" (Winnicott, 1956).

Perhaps Winnicott's most significant contribution to ontological psychoanalysis is his concept of "transitional objects and phenomena" (1971c), which he describes as

> an intermediate state of *experiencing,* to which inner reality and external life both contribute. It is an area that is not challenged, because no claim is made on its behalf except that it shall exist as a resting-place for the individual engaged in the perpetual human task of keeping inner and outer reality separate yet interrelated.
>
> (p. 2, original emphasis)

The infant or child's capacity to develop a "state of being" (Winnicott, 1971c, p. 14) bound up with experiencing transitional objects and phenomena requires a corresponding state of being on the part of the mother (or the analyst) in which

> *it is a matter of agreement between us and the baby that we will never ask the question: "Did you conceive of this* [object] *or was it presented to you from without?" The important point is that no decision on this point is expected. The question is not to be formulated.*
>
> (Winnicott, 1971c, p. 12, original emphasis)

The state of being underlying transitional phenomena is paradoxical in nature:

> In health the infant creates what is in fact lying around waiting
> to be found. But in health *the object is created, not found* ... This
> has to be accepted as a paradox, and not solved by a restatement
> that, by its cleverness, seems to eliminate the paradox.
>
> (Winnicott, 1963, p. 181,
> original emphasis)

This state of being underlies "the intense experiencing that belongs
to the arts and to religion and to imaginative living" (Winnicott,
1971c, p. 14). (When Winnicott speaks of the mother–infant relationship, he is using this as a metaphor that includes not only the
mother–infant relationship, but also the analyst–patient relationship,
as well as every other significant relationship experienced by infants,
children, and adults.)

Also prominent among Winnicott's contributions to ontological
psychoanalysis is his conception of the state of being that resides at
the core of the self:

> the non-communicating central self, for ever immune from the
> reality principle [immune to the need to respond to anything
> external to the self], and for ever silent. Here communication
> is not non-verbal; it is, like the music of the spheres, absolutely
> personal. It belongs to being alive. And in health, it is out of
> this that communication naturally arises.
>
> (1963, p. 192)

This state of being that lies at the core of the self constitutes an
impenetrable (utterly unknowable) mystery that is the source both
of lively communicating and absolute silence. The silence at the core
of the self is not verbal in nature, but what makes the state of being
at our core unimaginable is the fact that it is also "not non-verbal."
Silence that is neither verbal nor non-verbal is beyond human com-
prehension. "It is, like the music of the spheres, absolutely personal." The metaphor of the music of the spheres is derived from
Pythagoras's fifth-century BC conception of the music produced by
the movement of celestial bodies, a music of perfect harmony, but
inaudible to humankind. How better to describe the inconceivable
secret that each of us keeps at the core of our being, a secret that is
"absolutely personal. It belongs to being alive."

Bion's contributions to ontological psychoanalysis

As I read Bion, throughout his opus, he is principally an ontological thinker. Just as Winnicott shifted the focus of analysis from play to playing, Bion shifted the analytic focus from (the understanding of) dreams to (the experience of) dreaming (which, for Bion, is synonymous with doing unconscious psychological work [cf. Ogden, 2007a]).

Bion insists that, as psychoanalysts, we must shed the desire to understand, and instead engage as fully as possible in the *experience of being* with the patient. We must "cultivate a watchful avoidance of memory" (Bion, 1967, p. 137) because memory is what we think we know based on what no longer exists, and is no longer knowable. And we must renounce "desires for results, 'cure,' or even understanding" (p. 137). Both memory of what we think we know and desire for understanding of what has not yet occurred (and consequently is unknowable) are a "hindrance to the psychoanalyst's intuition of the reality [of what is occurring *in the present moment* of a session] with which he must be at one" (1967, p. 136). This is Bion's brand of ontological thinking: being has supplanted understanding; the analyst does not come to know or understand or comprehend or apprehend the reality of what is happening in the session, he "intuits" it, he *becomes* "at one" with it, he *is* fully present in *experiencing* the present moment.

Bion's (1962a, b) conception of "reverie" also reflects his ontological bent. Reverie (waking-dreaming) is *a state of being* that entails making oneself unconsciously receptive to experiencing what is so disturbing to the patient (or infant) that he is unable to "dream" (to do unconscious psychological work with) the experience. The analyst's (or mother's) reveries—waking-dreaming, which often takes the form of his most mundane, quotidian thoughts (Ogden, 1997a, b)—constitute a way in which the analyst (or mother) unconsciously experiences something like the patient's (or infant's) unthinkable, undreamable experience. In the analytic setting, the analyst makes available to the patient the transformed (dreamt) version of the patient's "undreamt" or partially dreamt experience by speaking (or relating in other forms) *from*, not *about*, reverie experience (Ogden, 1994).

Bion speaks in terms of states of being when he describes psychic health and psychopathology, for example, psychosis is a state of being in which the individual "cannot go to sleep and cannot wake up" (Bion, 1962a, p. 7).

I view Bion's (1962a) theory of alpha-function as a metaphor for the transformation of beta-elements (raw sense impressions that are bodily responses to experience, but which do not yet constitute meaning, much less *being* oneself) into alpha-elements, which comprise components of subjectless being, much like Winnicott's "going on being." Alpha-elements are linked with one another in the process of producing "dream-thoughts," which in turn are used in the process of dreaming. Dreaming is the psychic event in which the individual becomes a subject experiencing his own being. When, in severe forms of psychopathology (which I will describe in the clinical portion of this chapter), alpha-function ceases to process sense impressions, not only does the individual lose the capacity to create meaning, he also loses the capacity to experience himself as alive and real.

For me, Bion's ontological thinking comes alive in a particularly vivid way in his "Clinical Seminars" (1987). I will offer a few examples that hold particular importance to me. To a presenter who is worried by the "mistakes" he made with a patient, Bion comments that only "*after* you have become qualified and have finished your own analysis—then you have a chance to find out who you really are [as an analyst]" (1987, p. 34; see also Gabbard and Ogden, 2009, on becoming an analyst). Here, Bion is differentiating between learning how to "do analysis" and the experience of *being and becoming* "who you really are" as an analyst.

I would add that becoming an analyst involves developing an "analytic style" (Ogden, 2007b) that is uniquely one's own, as opposed to adopting "a technique" handed down from previous generations of analysts. In so doing, we "invent psychoanalysis" (see Chapter 3) for each patient and develop the capacity to respond spontaneously in the moment, sometimes in words, at other times non-verbally. There are times when spontaneous response takes the form of action. Such actions are unique to a particular moment of the analysis of a particular patient; they are not generalizable to work with other patients. When asked, for example, if I would go to a patient's home for a session, or take a severely ill patient in my car to a hospital, or meet with the patient's family, or accept a patient's gift, I say, "It all depends."

One of Bion's (1987) comments to a presenter entails a particularly vivid example of his ontological thinking. The presenter says that his psychotic patient told him he had a dream. Bion asks, "Why does he say they are dreams?" (p. 142). The presenter, nonplussed, replies, "He simply tells me so" (p. 142).

A bit later, Bion describes the way in which he might have spoken to the patient, a manner that addresses the patient's state of being:

> So why does the patient come to see a psycho-analyst and say he had a dream? I can imagine myself saying to a patient, "Where were you last night? What did you see?" If the patient told me he didn't see anything—he just went to bed—I would say, "Well, I still want to know where you went and what you saw."
>
> (p. 142)

Here, Bion is imagining talking with a patient in a way that focuses not on the content of what the patient is calling a dream, but on the state of being of the patient—Where did you go? "Where were you?" Who were you? Who did you become when you got into bed? This response strikes me as a remarkably adept way of talking with a psychotic patient about his state of being while asleep.

Ontological psychoanalysis and object-relations theory

For object-relations theorists (for example, Freud in some of his writings [cf. Ogden, 2002], Klein, Fairbairn, and Guntrip), alterations of unconscious internal object relationships (and the resultant change in relationships with external objects) constitute the medium through which psychic change occurs.

For Freud (1917), Klein (1946), Fairbairn (1940, 1944, 1958), and Guntrip (1961, 1969), to name only a few "object-relations theorists," internal object relationships take the form of relationships among split-off and repressed parts of the ego. For Fairbairn, the relationships among the repressed, split-off parts of the ego are internalizations of the unsatisfactory aspects of the real relationship with the mother. The internal object world is a closed system of addictive relationships with tantalizing and rejecting internal objects (Fairbairn, 1944). A driving force for the individual, from infancy onward, is the wish to transform the internalized unsatisfactory object-relationships with the mother into satisfactory relationships characterized by feelings of love for and from the mother, and the feeling that she recognizes and accepts one's love (cf. Ogden, 2010). It is the patient's release from the closed system of internal object relationships and entry into the world of real external objects that is the aim of psychoanalysis (Fairbairn, 1958).

For Klein (1961, 1975), who is an object–relations theorist of a sort different from Fairbairn, the patient's anxieties are derived from the dangers emanating from phantasied internal object relationships. Unconscious phantasies (the psychic manifestations of life and death instincts) are often concerned with what is occurring inside the body of the mother/analyst, for instance, attacks on the babies or the father's penis inside the mother. These primitive anxieties are manifested in the transference and interpreted in such a way that they ring true to the patient and help diminish the patient's persecutory and depressive anxieties which are impeding psychic growth.

Klein's object–relations theory differs from Fairbairn's in many ways. Their primary difference lies in the way Fairbairn views internal object relationships as internalizations of actual unsatisfactory experience in the mother–infant relationship, while Klein views internal object relationships as unconscious phantasies derived from the infant's experience of envy (the principal psychic manifestation of the death instinct).

I do not view Winnicott and Bion as object–relations theorists. (Reference to internal object relationships is rare in the work of both of these authors.) They are not primarily concerned with understanding and interpreting the pathological internal object relationships in which the patient is ensnared. Their focus is primarily on the range of states of being experienced by the patient (and the analyst) and the states of being the patient (or analyst) is unable to experience. For object–relations theorists, psychic growth involves freeing oneself from the persecutory and depressive anxieties generated in his internal object world (Klein) or freeing oneself from the addictive ties between internal objects, so one can engage in relationships with real external objects (Fairbairn and Guntrip). As I have discussed, for Winnicott and Bion, the most fundamental human need is that of *being and becoming more fully oneself, which to my mind, involves becoming more fully present and alive to one's thoughts, feelings, and bodily states; becoming better able to sense one's own unique creative potentials and finding forms in which to develop them; feeling that one is speaking one's own ideas with a voice of one's own; becoming a larger*

21

person (perhaps more generous, more compassionate, more loving, more open) in one's relationships with others; developing more fully a humane and just value system and set of ethical standards; and so on.

Not only are unconscious internal object relationships rarely mentioned by Winnicott and Bion, Winnicott in his late work (for example, *Playing and Reality* [1971d]) makes little explicit mention of the unconscious, and Bion creates a new conception of the nature of the unconscious. *States of being infuse every aspect of oneself; they transcend the divide between conscious and unconscious aspects of mind, between being asleep and being awake, between dream-life and waking life, between the psychotic and non-psychotic parts of the personality.*

Clinical illustrations of ontological psychoanalysis

"Ontological psychoanalysis" is a conception of psychoanalysis which, like every other understanding of psychoanalysis, can be hardened into a mindless ideology. "Ontological psychoanalysis" is a dimension of analytic theory and practice that coexists with many other dimensions (ways of thinking), including, but not limited to, an epistemological dimension. But as I have said earlier, it is also true that, for me, there are large sectors of analytic thinking and practice that are predominantly ontological or epistemological in nature.

I will now briefly illustrate clinically what I have in mind when I refer to the ontological dimension of psychoanalysis. It must be kept in mind in the clinical portion of this chapter that my interventions are meant as illustrations that pertain only to a given patient at a particular moment in his or her analytic experience, and *do not represent an analytic technique*. I believe that an analyst's rigid adherence to any set of rules of clinical practice (for instance, a technique associated with a school of psychoanalysis) not only feels impersonal to the patient, but also limits the analyst's capacity to be creative in working with his or her patients. I speak with each patient in a way that is different from the way I speak to any other patient (see Chapter 3).

Haven't you had enough of that by now?

The patient, a 30-year-old man, several years into the analysis, had a falling out with his father and had not spoken to him for a year. We had discussed this situation in many forms over the years. Just before the end of a session, I said, "Haven't you had enough of that by now?"

In this fragment of an analytic session, I told the patient in a highly condensed way that continuing to not talk to his father was a *way of being* that no longer reflected who the patient had become in the course of the previous years of analysis. Not talking with his father may have suited the person who the patient once was, but not the person he is now.

The patient called his father that evening. His father, too, had changed and welcomed hearing from his son. The patient told me in the closing months of the analysis that he would never forget my saying to him, "Haven't you had enough of that by now?" That moment in the analysis to which he was referring was less an experience of arriving at an understanding, and more an experience that altered something fundamental to who the patient was.

Of course you are

Ms. L, at the beginning of our initial analytic meeting, sat in her chair, her face drained of color. She burst into tears and said, "I'm terrified by being here." I replied, without planning to do so, "Of course you are."

Spontaneously responding in the way I did (saying something I had never said to any other patient) felt to me in the moment to be a way of being fully accepting of the patient's terrified state. Had I asked, "What's frightening you?" or "Tell me more," I think that the patient very likely would have felt that I was backing away from the intensity of her feeling by asking her to engage in secondary process thinking aimed at finding reasons and explanations, as opposed to *experiencing* the patient's way of introducing herself to me (telling me who she was at that moment). (See also Chapter 3 for further exploration of this experience.)

Do you watch TV?

I met with Jim on a long-term adolescent inpatient ward five times a week. He did not come to the sessions on his own and had to be brought by one of the nurses. Jim did not object to seeing me, but when the two of us were seated in the small room on the ward used for psychotherapy, he seemed not to know why the two of us were sitting there. He was silent most of the time. I learned that asking him questions led only to perfunctory one-word replies.

As time went on, he began to talk with me about events on the ward—new patients arriving, others leaving—but the words he used sounded imitative of things he had heard other people say at ward group meetings and community meetings. I said to him, "It's hard to know if you're coming or going." He looked bewildered.

I found the sessions trying and had the feeling that I did not know the first thing about how to work with this patient, or with any other patient, for that matter.

About five months into the analysis, Jim was brought to his session walking in a listless way. His face was utterly expressionless; his eyes were like the eyes of a dead bird. He said to no one in particular, "Jim is lost and gone forever."

I felt something of relief that the thin charade covering an immense psychic catastrophe was over, but I also felt that a psychic death had occurred which could easily become actual suicide. A patient on the ward, a year earlier, had committed suicide, and the memory of this event had become part of the (usually unspoken) culture of the ward.

I said, "Jim has been lost and gone for a very long time, and only now is the word out."

He looked into the glare of the reflected sunlight in the Plexiglas window, his eyes unfocused.

I was silent for some time feeling the immense emptiness of what was happening. As this was occurring, I began to feel strongly that the danger of suicide on the ward was grossly underestimated and the ward should become a locked ward which the patients could only leave with the permission of the staff, and usually accompanied by a staff member. I became aware of the distance that I was creating between the patient and me. He was now a "dangerous" patient who frightened me. I was now "managing" him, a person who had become a thing.

After some time had passed in the session, I noticed that the usual background noise of my mind—the thoughts that came and went, the "peripheral vision" of reverie, even the bodily feelings of my heart pumping, my breath moving, were absent. I felt frightened that not only had Jim disappeared, I too was disappearing. Everything was becoming unreal—the small room in which we were seated ceased being a room; it had become a collection of shapes, colors, and textures; everything seemed arbitrary. I felt the terror of drowning, but at the same time, I was an indifferent observer, simply watching myself drowning.

As the session continued, I was reminded of a frightening experience I had had as an adolescent when, alone in the kitchen after dinner, I repeated the word *napkin*, out loud, over and over again until it became a mere sound, no longer having any tie to the thing it once named. I was at first intrigued by this phenomenon when I began the "experiment," but quickly became frightened that if I were to do with other words what I was doing with the word *napkin*, I would lose the ability to speak or think or have any connection with anyone or any thing. For many years after that event, the sound *nap* followed by the sound *kin* did not name anything, they were simply sounds that caused me to doubt the stability of my connection to anyone, even to myself. In the session with Jim, I felt momentarily relieved to have a mind that could remember a past that was continuous with the present, but this relief was only a momentary respite from my fear that if I stayed in the room with Jim, I would lose myself.

I dreaded the daily meetings with Jim. For several weeks, we sat together, mostly in empty silence. I did not ask him questions. I, now and again, tried to describe what I was experiencing. I said to him, "Sitting here feels like being nowhere and being no one." He made no response, not even the slightest change of facial expression.

For the six weeks following Jim's telling me he was lost and gone forever, I felt adrift and directionless with him. To my great surprise, in the middle of a session, Jim said with an expressionless voice, as if to nobody, "Do you watch TV?"

I took his question not as a symbolic comment on feeling like a machine that displayed images of people talking to one another, but as his way of asking me, "Who are you?"

I said, "Yes, I do. I watch quite a lot of TV."

Jim made no response.

After a while, I said, "Have you ever seen someone strike a match in a place that's completely dark, maybe a cave, and everything lights up, so you can see everything—or at least a lot—and then, a moment later, everything gets dark again, but not as dark as it had been."

Jim did not reply, but it did not feel to me that the silence we returned to was as empty as it had been.

I looked at my watch and found that we had gone half an hour past the end of the 50-minute session. I said, "It's time to stop." He looked at me and said, "Is it?" It seemed to me that he was correcting me: the experience we had had was not one that could be measured in, or dictated by, "clock time."

In the first of the sessions I have described, I was for quite a long time completely immersed in a state of losing my sense of being someone. Jim and I were "lost and gone forever," and initially we were each absolutely alone in that state—we did not exist for one another, any more than we existed for ourselves. I refrained from asking the patient questions about what was happening or what might have led him to feel as he did. I simply experienced a terrifying sense of losing myself, which was essential if I was to ever be of any use to him. In not being anyone, I was experiencing something akin to what he was feeling in the session, and probably for the entirety of his life.

My reverie about my own experience as an adolescent helped me, at least for a moment, to be both in the situation with the patient and to bring to it some of my own sense of living at the very edge, *but not over the edge*, of losing myself.

The patient's asking me, about six weeks into this period of the analysis, "Do you watch TV?" felt to me as if I was hearing a dog speak. His addressing me, acknowledging me, was astounding. I was not the least bit inclined to take up possible symbolic meanings of watching TV, for to do so would have decimated the living experience that was occurring, an event having everything to do with being, and little to do with understanding.

I told the patient, in response to his question, that I watched quite a lot of TV. But the more important part of my response to his question took the form of my *describing* (not explaining) by means of a metaphor something of the state of being I felt was occurring: the sensory experience of the striking of a match and illuminating for a moment what had been invisible (the two of us as separate people), followed by a feeling that the darkness was not quite as absolute as it had been.

How to begin?

I have for most of my career been fascinated by the initial analytic meeting, by which I mean the very first time I meet the patient

(Ogden, 1992). Many of the clinical examples I have provided in this chapter and in other analytic papers have been taken from initial sessions. In writing this chapter, I have come to appreciate an aspect of the initial meeting that I have not been able to name until now. I now suspect that the depth and intimacy and suspense I feel in the first meeting derives in part from the fact that in that meeting, for the patient, one question is of more importance than any other: "*Who is this person* who I hope will help me." And I am asking, "*Who is this person* who is coming to me for help?" These are fundamental ontological questions. Responses to these questions arise in the experience with one another that unfolds. I hope that at the end of the meeting, if the patient asks how I practice psychoanalysis, I can say, "Just as you've seen today."

I will describe an initial meeting that illustrates a way a patient in effect asked me, "Who are you?" and the way I replied.

Mr. D told me in his first session that he would never begin a session. He had seen six previous analysts all of whom had unilaterally terminated the analysis. In these aborted analyses, the analyst had refused to begin sessions, as the patient had asked them to do, and instead used "hackneyed analytic tricks" such as beginning the session by asking him what it feels like not to be able to begin the session. If we were to begin a therapy, it would be up to me, Mr. D told me, to begin each of the sessions. I said that that would be fine with me, but it might take me some time to begin the sessions because I would begin each meeting by telling him what it felt like being with him on that particular day. He said that that would be okay with him, but there was thick skepticism in his voice regarding my willingness to carry through with what I was promising.

In this exchange, the patient and I were introducing ourselves to one another, showing more than telling who we were at that moment, and who we were in the process of *becoming with one another.* The patient was asking me to respect his way of being, his way of allaying his terrors, and I was showing him that I honored his request that I be the analyst he needed me to be.

In the course of the analysis, I began the sessions. The patient was gradually able to reclaim parts of himself, parts of his unlived life as a child, which had been too brutal, too frightening to experience at the time they occurred. (See Ogden, 1995, for a detailed discussion of this case.)

Because she was dead

A clinical experience in a group setting conveys a good deal of what I mean by the ontological dimension of psychoanalysis. The experience occurred in a "Balint Group" in which I participated for a year at the Tavistock Clinic. The group of seven GPs (General Practitioners) met weekly with the psychoanalyst who led the group for two years to discuss their clinical work. In the group in which I participated, each meeting began with the analyst asking, "Who's got a case?" In one of these meetings, a GP in his mid–40s said that he had received a call from a patient saying that her elderly mother had died in her sleep at home. Both the woman who called and her mother had been patients in his practice for many years. He told his patient that he would come by that afternoon. When he arrived, the daughter took him to her mother's room where he examined her.

The GP said he then called the mortuary. The analyst asked, "Why did you do that?" The GP, puzzled by the question, said, "Because she was dead."

The analyst said, "Why not have a cup of tea with the daughter?"

Those words—"Why not have a cup of tea with the daughter?"— have stayed with me for the 44 years since I heard them. Such a simple statement captures the essence of what I mean by the practice of ontological psychoanalysis. The group leader was pointing out that the GP took haste in getting the body of the mother out of the apartment, and in that way, foreclosed the opportunity to *live the experience with the daughter* by simply being with her in that apartment where her mother lay dead in the bedroom. (For further discussion of this experience, see Ogden 2006.)

What do you want to be when you grow up?

I will close this chapter by describing an experience with a patient that holds great importance to me.

Mr. C, a patient with cerebral palsy, had begun work with me in a twice-weekly psychotherapy because he was in great distress, with intense suicidal thoughts, in response to unreciprocated love of a woman, Ms. Z (who suffered from no physical disabilities). He described how, as a child, his mother had thrown shoes from her closet at him to keep the "slobbering monster" away from her. Mr. C walked in awkward, lumbering strides and spoke in poorly articulated

28

speech. He was a college graduate who worked well at a demanding technical job. In the course of working together for some time, I became very fond of Mr. C and when he bellowed in pain, with mucus dripping from his nose and tears streaming down his face, I felt a form of love for him that I would later feel for my infant sons.

Several years into our work, after considerable change had occurred regarding his desperate longing for the love of Ms. Z, Mr. C told me a dream: "Not much happened in the dream. I was myself with my cerebral palsy washing my car and enjoying listening to music on the car radio that I had turned up loud."

The dream was remarkable in that it was the first time Mr. C, in telling me a dream, not only mentioned the fact that he had cerebral palsy, he seemed to fully accept it as a part of who he was: "I was myself with cerebral palsy." How better to recognize and accept himself for who he was in a loving way? No longer the monster he had once felt himself to be, he was, in the dream, a baby being joyfully bathed and sung to by a mother who took delight in him just as he was. The dream was not a manic picture of succeeding in winning the love of an unreachable mother, it was a part of ordinary life: "Not much happened in the dream."

I had not the slightest inclination to talk with Mr. C about my understanding of the dream. I said to him, "What a wonderful dream that was." (For a detailed discussion of this clinical work, see Ogden, 2010.)

Being able to recognize and tenderly accept himself, just as he was, might be thought of as Mr. C's response (at that moment) to the question, "What do you want to be when you grow up?" Himself.

References

Balint, M. (1992). *The Basic Fault: Therapeutic Aspects of Regression*. London: Routledge.

Berman, E. (2001). Psychoanalysis and life. *The Psychoanalytic Quarterly*, 70:35–65.

Bion, W. R. (1962a). *Learning from Experience*. London: Tavistock.

Bion, W. R. (1962b). A theory of thinking. In *Second Thoughts*. New York: Aronson, 1967, pp. 110–119.

Bion, W. R. (1967). Notes on memory and desire. In *Wilfred Bion: Los Angeles Seminars and Supervision*, edited by J. Aguayo & B. Malin. London: Karnac, 2013, pp. 136–138.

Bion, W. R. (1987). Clinical seminars. In *Clinical Seminars and Other Works*, edited by F. Bion. London: Karnac, pp. 1–240.

Civitarese, G. (2010). *The Intimate Room: Theory and Technique of the Analytic Field*. P. Slotkin (trans). London: Routledge.

Civitarese, G. (2016). Truth as immediacy and unison: A new common ground in psychoanalysis? Commentary on essays addressing "Is truth relevant?" *The Psychoanalytic Quarterly*, 85:449–502.

Eshel, O. (2004). Let it be and become me: Notes on containing, identification, and the possibility of being. *Contemporary Psychoanalysis*, 40:323–351.

Fairbairn, W. R. D. (1940). Schizoid factors in the personality. In *Psychoanalytic Studies of the Personality*. London: Routledge, pp. 3–27.

Fairbairn, W. R. D. (1944). Endopsychic structure considered in terms of object relationships. In *Psychoanalytic Studies of the Personality*. London: Routledge and Kegan Paul, 1952, pp. 82–132.

Fairbairn, W. R. D. (1958). On the nature and aims of psychoanalytical treatment. *The International Journal of Psychoanalysis*, 39:374–385.

Ferro, A. (2011). *Avoiding Emotions, Living Emotions*. I. Harvey (trans.) London: Routledge.

Freud, S. (1912). Recommendations to physicians practicing psycho-analysis. S.E. 12.

Freud, S. (1917). Mourning and melancholia. S.E. 14.

Freud, S. (1923). Two encyclopaedia articles. S.E. 18.

Freud, S. (1926). *Inhibitions, Symptoms and Anxiety*. S.E. 20.

Freud, S. (1933). *New Introductory Lectures on Psychoanalysis*. XXXI. The dissection of the psychical personality. S.E. 22.

Gabbard, G. O. (2009). What is a "good enough" termination? *Journal of the American Psychoanalytic Association*, 57:575–594.

Gabbard, G. O. & Ogden, T. H. (2009). On becoming a psychoanalyst. *The International Journal of Psychoanalysis*, 90:311–327.

Greenberg, J. (2016). Editor's introduction: Is truth relevant? *The Psychoanalytic Quarterly*, 85:269–274.

Grinberg, L. (1980). The closing page of the psychoanalytic treatment of adults and the goals of psychoanalysis: "The search for truth about oneself." *The International Journal of Psychoanalysis*, 61:25–37.

Grotstein, J. S. (2000). Psychoanalytic subjects. In *Who Is the Dreamer Who Dreams the Dream?* Hillsdale, NJ: The Analytic Press, pp. 101–142.

Guntrip, H. (1961). *Personality Structure and Human Interaction*. New York: International Universities Press.

Guntrip, H. (1969). *Schizoid Phenomena, Object Relations and the Self.* New York: International Universities Press.

Klein, M. (1932). *The Psycho-Analysis of Children.* New York: Humanities Press, 1969.

Klein, M. (1946). Notes on some schizoid mechanisms. In *Envy and Gratitude and Other Works, 1946–1953.* New York: Delacorte, 1975, pp. 1–24.

Klein, M. (1955). The psycho-analytic play technique: Its history and significance. In *Envy and Gratitude and Other Works, 1946–1963.* New York: Delacorte Press/Seymour Lawrence, 1975, pp. 122–140.

Klein, M. (1961). *Narrative of a Child Analysis.* New York: Delacorte Press/ Seymour Lawrence.

Klein, M. (1975). *Envy and Gratitude and Other Works, 1946–1963.* New York: Delacorte Press/Seymour Lawrence.

Laing, R. D. (1960). *The Divided Self.* London: Penguin.

Laplanche, J. & Pontalis, J.-B. (1973). *The Language of Psycho-Analysis.* New York: Norton.

Levine, H. (2016). Psychoanalysis and the problem of truth. *The Psychoanalytic Quarterly,* 85:391–410.

Milner, M. (1950). *On Not Being Able to Paint.* London: Routledge, 2010.

Ogden, T. H. (1992). The initial analytic meeting. *Psychoanalytic Inquiry,* 12:225–247.

Ogden, T. H. (1994). The analytic third: working with intersubjective clinical facts. *The International Journal of Psychoanalysis,* 75:3–20.

Ogden, T. H. (1995). Analysing forms of aliveness and deadness of the transference-countertransference. *The International Journal of Psychoanalysis,* 76:695–710.

Ogden, T. H. (1997a). Reverie and interpretation. *The Psychoanalytic Quarterly,* 66:567–595.

Ogden, T. H. (1997b). *Reverie and Interpretation: Sensing Something Human.* Northvale, NJ: Jason Aronson.

Ogden, T. H. (2002). A new reading of the origins of object-relations theory. *The International Journal of Psychoanalysis,* 83:767–782.

Ogden, T. H. (2006). On teaching psychoanalysis. *The International Journal of Psychoanalysis,* 87:1069–1085.

Ogden, T. H. (2007a). On talking-as-dreaming. *The International Journal of Psychoanalysis,* 88:575–589.

Ogden, T. H. (2007b). Elements of analytic style: Bion's clinical seminars. *The International Journal of Psychoanalysis,* 88:1185–1200.

Ogden, T. H. (2010). Why read Fairbairn? *The International Journal of Psychoanalysis*, 91:101–118.

Searles, H. (1986). *Collected Papers on Schizophrenia and Related Subjects*. New York: International Universities Press.

Semrad, E. V. & Day, M. (1966). Group psychotherapy. *Journal of the American Psychoanalytic Association*, 14:591–618.

Stern, D. N., Sander, L. W., Nahum, J. P., Harrison, A. M., Lyons-Ruth, K., Morgan, A. C., Bruschweiler-Stern, N. & Tronick, E. Z. (1998). Non-interpretive mechanisms in psychoanalytic therapy: The "something more" than interpretation. *The International Journal of Psychoanalysis*, 79:903–921.

Sullivan, H. S. (1962). *Schizophrenia as a Human Process*. New York: Norton.

Will, O. A. (1968). The reluctant patient, the unwanted psychotherapist—and coercion. *Contemporary Psychoanalysis*, 5:1–31.

Williams, P. (2019). Isolation. *Psychoanalytic Dialogues*, 29:1–12.

Winnicott, D. W. (1949). Mind and its relation to the psyche-soma. In *Through Paediatrics to Psychoanalysis*. New York: Basic Books, 1958, pp. 243–254.

Winnicott, D. W. (1956). Primary maternal preoccupation. In *Through Paediatrics to Psychoanalysis*. New York: Basic Books, pp. 300–305.

Winnicott, D. W. (1963). Communicating and not communicating leading to a study of certain opposites. In *The Maturational Processes and the Facilitating Environment*. New York: International Universities Press, 1965, pp. 179–192.

Winnicott, D. W. (1969). The use of an object and relating through identifications. In *Playing and Reality*. New York: Basic Books, pp. 86–94.

Winnicott, D. W. (1971a). Playing: A theoretical statement. In *Playing and Reality*. New York: Basic Books, pp. 38–52.

Winnicott, D. W. (1971b). Dreaming, fantasying, and living. In *Playing and Reality*. New York: Basic Books, pp. 26–37.

Winnicott, D. W. (1971c). Transitional objects and transitional phenomena. In *Playing and Reality*. New York: Basic Books, pp. 1–25.

Winnicott, D. W. (1971d). *Playing and Reality*. New York: Basic Books.

2

THE FEELING OF REAL

On Winnicott's "Communicating and not communicating leading to a study of certain opposites"

In "Communicating and not communicating leading to a study of certain opposites" (Winnicott, 1963a)—one of his most important and daring, and for me, one of his most difficult papers—Winnicott sets himself the task of describing the state of being at our central core. To do so involves finding a way to gesture toward the inexpressible, the ineffable, to communicate something of the mystery of being, which is "absolutely personal" (p. 192) to each of us. (Unless otherwise indicated, page numbers refer to Winnicott [1963a].) Winnicott states that he has allowed himself "a great deal of freedom in following trains of thought" (p. 192) in writing this paper. He gives himself room to try out a series of concepts and metaphors, finally arriving at a form of thinking and a use of language that I imagine he did not anticipate when he set out to write this paper.

The non–communicating self

Winnicott opens the paper in a rather choppy way: an epigraph from Keats—"*Every point of thought is the centre of an intellectual world*" (p. 179, original emphasis)—followed by an admission that his paper "contains only one idea, a rather obvious idea at that" (p. 179); then an apology for "only gradually" (p. 179) getting to the point of the paper; and finally, this striking personal comment:

DOI: 10.4324/9781003228462-2

Starting from no fixed place I soon came, while preparing this paper for a foreign society, to staking a claim, to my surprise, to the right not to communicate. This was a protest from the core of me to the frightening fantasy of being infinitely exploited. … In the language of this paper it is *the fantasy of being found.*

(p. 179, original emphasis)

This pair of questions—What does it mean to be found? and What does it mean not to be found?—recurs, like a leitmotif, to the very last sentences of the paper, each time framing these questions in a slightly different way, each time arriving at a slightly different conception of communication at the core of the self.

Winnicott tells us that before going on to the topic of communication it is necessary to "restate some of my views on object-relating" (p. 179). I will not explore these "restated ideas" here, but will discuss a number of them in the course of the current chapter. (See Abram, 1996, for a thoughtful discussion of the development of Winnicott's theory of object-relating, which evolved until it reached its final form in "The use of an object and relating through identifications" [1969].)

As Winnicott turns his attention to a psychoanalytic study of communication, he does so in a way that I find very difficult to follow, in part because of the ambiguity and indefiniteness of the words (for example, the words *explicit*, *implicit*, and *dumb*); in part because the syntax of the sentences is complex and confusing (perhaps intentionally so); and in part because the term *subjective object* is reinvented here and takes on meaning solely by the way it is used in this passage (a meaning that changes as the paper progresses):

In so far as the object is subjective, *so far is it unnecessary for communication with it to be explicit.* In so far as the object is objectively perceived, communication is either explicit or else dumb. Here then appear two *new* things, the individual's use and enjoyment of modes of communication, and the individual's non-communicating self, or the personal core of the self that is a true isolate.

(p. 182, original emphasis)

I struggle with these sentences each time I read them. It seems to me (at this moment) that Winnicott is making a first pass, not only at a theory of communicating and not communicating, but as importantly, at a theory of the nature of the state of being at our core. He begins this passage by saying that to the degree that the object is a subjective object (an object "in the area of omnipotence as a living experience" [p. 182]), communication need not be explicit (which seems here to mean it need not be symbolic communication). Communication with objects objectively perceived (external objects) may be explicit (perhaps symbolic) or dumb (mute, not requiring words to convey symbolic meaning—perhaps communication in the form of a change in facial expression that conveys an emotional state).

The final sentence of the passage makes a large leap. Winnicott writes, "Here then appear two *new* things," which seems to refer to the appearance *two new states of being* in the wake of the achievement of communication with subjective objects and with objective objects. The term *appear* seems to me to be carefully chosen in that it does not denote a cause-and-effect relationship between the two new things, rather it suggests concurrent developments. One of the "*new* things," new states of being, that arises is the use and enjoyment of the experience of being able to communicate with a world experienced as external to oneself. The description of the other state of being that "appears" always comes as a surprise to me because it is so disproportionate with the first. The other existential state that arises constitutes a qualitatively different development: the creation of the core state of being human, which is "a non-communicating self, the personal core of the self that is a true isolate." Communication is not only "*unnecessary*," as Winnicott indicates at the opening of the passage, the absence of communication is an essential quality of this state of being. What is most personal is most isolated—its lines of communication with the external object world are cut absolutely. This quite extraordinary line of thought constitutes the first of a series of attempts Winnicott makes in his paper to describe the existential state that lies at the core of being human.

Winnicott then adds another layer of complexity to a situation already over-brimming with ideas he is in the process of developing:

> A complication in this line of argument arises out of the fact that the infant develops two kinds of relationships at one and the same time—that to the environment-mother and that to the object, which becomes the object-mother. The environment

35

mother is human, and the object-mother is a thing, although it is also the mother or part of her.

(pp. 182–183)

It seems to me that Winnicott is suggesting, but only suggesting, that there are two simultaneous modes of relating to the mother: (1) relating to the environment-mother as "human" (personal in a diffuse way, not located specifically in time or place), a form of relatedness that precedes even that of relating to subjective objects; and (2) relating to the object-mother, who has all the qualities of external "thing-ness," a thing with a definite place, size, shape, smell, movement, texture, and so on, all of which makes her real as a "not-me" thing, which holds the potential to become an external object if development proceeds in a healthy way.

In relation to the environment mother, "the infant could be said to communicate simply by going on being, ... but this scarcely deserves the epithet communication" (p. 183). In the final, apparently throwaway clause of this sentence, Winnicott expands the concept of "communicating" to include communication with the mother-as-environment in the form of simply "going on being." The idea of communicating "simply by going on being" may represent the earliest, least differentiated state of being that the infant experiences, and that experience may lie at the core of the non-communicating, isolate self. (I twice use the word *may* because these are my extensions of Winnicott's thinking.)

Cul-de-sac communication

Winnicott makes use of opposites as a way of framing his ideas in this paper, more so than in his other major papers (as reflected in the title of the paper). The first of the opposites he introduces are two opposites of communication:

(1) A simple not-communicating.
(2) A not-communicating that is active or reactive. (p. 183)

Simple not-communicating is "like resting" (p. 183), and may return to communicating as naturally as sleep returns to wakefulness. "A not-communicating that is active or reactive" is an opposite of communication that has a direct bearing on what Winnicott considers the "one idea" of his paper and involves the use of a second set of metaphors to describe the state of being at the core of the self.

> In the psycho-pathology I need for my argument here the facil-
> itation [of the growth of the infant by the mother] has failed in
> some respect and in some degree, and in the matter of object-
> relating the infant has developed a split. By one half of the split
> the infant relates to the presenting object, and for this purpose
> there develops what I have called a false or compliant self.
>
> (p. 183)

The "object-relating" of the false self is neither an experience of relating to a subjective object nor to an object objectively perceived, but to "the presenting object," an object experienced solely as an impingement into the infant's sense of self—an object to be man-aged and deflected, not used for purposes of genuine communica-tion or psychic growth.

Winnicott continues:

> By the other half of the split [the half that is not the false self]
> the infant relates to a subjective object, or to mere phenomena
> based on body experiences, these being scarcely influenced by
> an objectively perceived world. (Clinically do we not see this
> in autistic rocking movements, for instance; and in the abstract
> picture [perhaps, I imagine, drawn by an autistic child in a
> therapy session] that is a cul-de-sac communication, and that
> has no general validity?)
>
> (p. 183)

Here, Winnicott is using the term *subjective objects* not to refer to objects that are in the process of becoming objects objectively per-ceived, objects emerging from "the area of omnipotence as a living experience" (p. 182); rather, in the case of severe psychopathology, a subjective object has the quality of "mere phenomena based on body experiences." I find this to be a remarkably expressive description of a form of pathological relatedness that is subjectless, objectless, and bodiless—"mere phenomena."

Winnicott finds in autistic rocking movement the pathological phenomenon "I need for my argument here" (p. 183). He views autistic rocking as sensation-dominated experience (devoid of a sense of self or body or other), a phenomenon that Tustin (1984) refers to as the experience of an "autistic shape," a felt presence which an outsider might call an experience of self-soothing, but for the autistic child there is no self to soothe or be soothed. For instance, an adult autistic patient I saw in analysis felt the need to be "wrapped in fog and the sound of fog horns"; another autistic patient required the "sensation of reading," which had nothing to do with the symbolic meaning of the words and sentences, which she forgot as soon as she read them.

The phrase "cul-de-sac communication" seems just right to describe the abstract drawings of an autistic child that have "no general validity," that is, the drawings of a child who has no capacity, and perhaps no wish, to symbolize, much less communicate anything to anyone. It is in these autistic dead ends, these non-symbolic creations, these "mere phenomena," not meant for anything or anyone, that Winnicott finds modes of experiencing that help to describe the nature of experience at the core of self.

All the sense of real

Winnicott moves directly from his conception of pathological cul-de-sac communication to a statement about early development in a state of health:

> In this way [by discussing the pathological split seen in autism] I am introducing the idea of a communication with subjective objects and at the same time the idea of an active non-communication with that which is objectively perceived by the infant. There seems to be no doubt that for all its futility from the observer's point of view, the cul-de-sac communication (communication with subjective objects) carries all the sense of real.
>
> (p. 184)

This, too, is quite a remarkable statement: the "cul-de-sac communication" seen in autism and other severe forms of psychopathology has a counterpart in "the more normal individual" (p. 184), which Winnicott is calling "communication with subjective objects." The concept of the "subjective object" as it is used here is being reinvented once again by Winnicott. Now, communicating with subjective objects is "cul-de-sac" communication (communication not meant for any external or internal object), but which nonetheless "carries all the sense of real."

Winnicott does not "explain" how "cul-de-sac communication (communication with subjective objects) carries all the sense of real," but his use of language serves to describe something of what this form of communicating and way of being *feels like*. Relatedness to subjective objects "carries"—as opposed to "conveys" or "generates" or "comprises"—all the sense of real. The meaning of the word *carries* includes the act not only of transporting, enduring, and containing, but also of being pregnant with. And communication with subjective objects is not simply pregnant with *the sense of real*, it is pregnant with *all the sense of real*—it is generously unbounded; it goes on endlessly; it encompasses everything. Moreover, communication with subjective objects does not carry all the sense of *what is real* or all the sense of *reality*. The idea of carrying *all the sense of what is real* applies to a way of experiencing external reality, as does the phrase *all the sense of reality*. Both of these alternative wordings—the sense of what is real and the sense of reality—are precise opposites of the conception of the state of being that Winnicott is attempting to convey: a state of being in which "there is no communication with the not-me world either way" (pp. 189–190), a state of being in which external reality is absolutely irrelevant.

The idea that "the cul-de-sac communication (communication with subjective objects) carries all the sense of real" constitutes one of the fundamental, but never stated, paradoxes of Winnicott's paper: the idea that "cul-de-sac communication" of a part of the self absolutely not-communicating with any other part of the self, is the part of the self that carries—is pregnant with—all the sense of real that one experiences in every aspect of being alive (for example, in one's body, in one's internal object relationships, in one's relationship with external reality). What is absolutely cut off is what is ubiquitous.

Winnicott continues:

> [I]n the cases of slighter illness, in which there is some pathology and some health, there must be expected an active non-communication (clinical withdrawal) because of the fact that communication so easily becomes linked with some degree of false or compliant object-relating; silent or secret

communication with subjective objects, carrying a sense of real, must periodically take over to restore balance.

(p. 184)

Communicating with subjective objects in the form of "clinical withdrawal," which I take to mean a state of mind that has the appearance of depression or schizoid introversion, is not actually an illness; in fact, it is the opposite of an illness. It is an assertion of the need to engage in communication with subjective objects "carrying a sense of real." Winnicott seems to be saying that "silent or secret communication with subjective objects" may in "cases of slighter illness" (which, as I see it, includes all of us) give way at times to excessive reliance on the false or compliant self. At such times, in my experience, one might recover the sense of real by means of dreaming (while awake or asleep), or solitude, or listening to music, or creative activity, or temporary withdrawal into healthy "sensation-dominated personal isolation" (Ogden, 1989, 1991).

Transitional phenomena and the sense of real

Winnicott interrupts the line of thought he has been tracing (silent communication with subjective objects) to address a different source of the sense of real.

> Real health need not be described only in terms of the residues in healthy persons of what might have been illness-patterns. One should be able to make a positive statement of the healthy use of non-communication in the establishment of the feeling of real. It may be necessary in doing so to speak in terms of man's cultural life, which is the adult equivalent of the transitional phenomena of infancy and early childhood, and in which area communication is made without reference to the object's state of being either subjective or objectively perceived.
> (p. 184)

Although Winnicott does not specify, I think that when he speaks of the "residues in healthy persons of what might have been illness-patterns," he is referring to the "cul-de-sac communications" seen in autistic patients. He feels he needs to make a "positive statement of the healthy use of non-communication in the establishment of the feeling of real" (p. 184). This sentiment is puzzling to me because the autistic psychopathology that Winnicott needed for his "argument," as I understand it, was used as a metaphor, a way of imagining the *apparent* pointlessness of communication at the core of the self.

Be that as it may, Winnicott, here, conceives of the feeling of real as arising from two sources: communication with subjective objects; and the healthy infant's and child's experience of transitional phenomena. Communication with transitional phenomena differs from communication with subjective objects in that communication in the area of transitional phenomena "is made without reference to the object's state of being subjectively or objectively perceived" (p. 184). Transitional phenomena belong not to an order of experience that is a combination of, or compromise between, reality and fantasy; rather, they belong to an order of experience that is *neither* fantasy nor reality, *neither* subjective nor objective. This is an area of experience that begins in childhood playing and continues throughout life in the "intermediate area" (p. 184) that comprises cultural life, including "art and religion" (p. 184). And yet, despite this assertion that the "feeling of real" arises in part from transitional phenomena, Winnicott returns, a bit later in the paper, to his original position that it is "the individual's communicating with subjective phenomena, which *alone* gives the feeling of real" (p. 188, emphasis added).

To my mind, transitional phenomena constitute a different order of experience from communication with subjective phenomena and generate a "feeling of real" that belongs to the area of imagination, while the sense of real carried by communication with subjective objects has more to do with something far more primal: our core sense of being originating when the "infant could be said to communicate simply by going on being" (p. 183). The distinction I am drawing may be the reason Winnicott wavers between viewing the "feeling of real" as arising from a single source (communication with subjective objects) or from two forms of experience (communication with subjective objects and communication with transitional phenomena).

Disaster not to be found, disaster to be found

Winnicott, then, for the first time since the opening paragraph, returns to the question of the relationship between the need to communicate and the need not to be found. As in the opening paragraph, this question is stated in what feels like a personal line of thought, though Winnicott makes no explicit reference to himself here.

> In the artist of all kinds I think one can detect an inherent dilemma, which belongs to the co-existence of two trends, the urgent need to communicate and the still more urgent need not to be found. This might account for the fact that we cannot conceive of an artist's coming to the end of the task that occupies his whole nature.
>
> (p. 185)

Again, the need to communicate (paradoxically) prevails over "*the still more urgent need* not to be found" (emphasis added). And at the same time, it is the need not to be found that seems to account for the inexhaustible nature of what inspires the artist to continue to create.

Winnicott goes on to offer, without introduction, a brief clinical vignette. The patient has a dream in which two of her women friends are customs officers examining her possessions with "absurd care" (p. 186). She then accidentally drives her car through a pane of glass. The patient, as a nine-year-old child, kept a private journal, which her mother read without her permission. The mother asked her daughter about the saying on the front page of her journal: "'What a man thinketh in his heart, so is he'" (p. 186). "It would have been alright," Winnicott comments, "for the mother to read the journal, if she had said nothing about it to her daughter" (p. 186).

Winnicott continues:

> Here is a picture of a girl establishing a private self that is not communicating, and at the same time wanting to communicate and to be found. It is a sophisticated game of hide-and-seek in which *it is joy to be hidden but disaster not to be found.*
>
> (p. 186, original emphasis)

The words, "*it is joy to be hidden but disaster not to be found,*" seem to stare across the page to the italicized portion of what may seem to be its opposite, an idea that Winnicott calls "my main point, the point of thought which is the centre of an intellectual world and of my paper" (p. 187):

> Although healthy persons communicate and enjoy communi-
> cating, the other fact is equally true, that *each individual is an
> isolate, permanently non-communicating, permanently unknown, in
> fact unfound*.
>
> (p. 187, original emphasis)

Winnicott makes no comment concerning whether these two statements are contradictory, or paradoxical, or a pair of opposites: it is
"*disaster not to be found*," in the first statement; in the second, it is
essential to remain "*unfound*." As I spend time with these two statements, they seem less and less to constitute a paradox, a contradic-
tion, or even a pair of opposites. The words *found* and *unfound* in the
two statements refer, I think, to states of being involved in quite different sorts of experiences. To my mind, in the first, the word *found*
refers to a state of *being recognized, but not exposed*. The nine-year-old
girl in the clinical vignette was exposed by her mother. It would
have been all right "for the mother to read the journal, if she had
said nothing" (p. 186).

"It is a sophisticated game of hide-and-seek": the need to be recognized, but not exposed is universal, but perhaps most painfully
evident in latency-aged children and adolescents, when in health, it
is a joy to hide from one's parents (while personal identity is being
formed, and along with it, a readiness to be recognized), and at the
same time they have an intense need to be looked for, to be sought
out, not to be neglected, not to be allowed to disappear, not to have
to go to violent destructive and self-destructive extremes to be seen.

The word *unfound* in the second of the two statements—"*each
individual is an isolate, permanently non-communicating, permanently
unknown, in fact unfound*"—refers to a state of being characterizing
"the deepest layers of the ... personality" (p. 189), the core self,
where to be found is to be violated to a degree that makes "rape, and
being eaten by cannibals ... mere bagatelles" (p. 187).

The seemingly contradictory pair of statements under discussion,
when taken together, refer to powerful competing forces in each
of us: the need to be an isolate and the need to be recognized, but
not exposed. This is true of human experience from the earliest
stages of development when in health the mother provides the infant

and child an "environment [that] enables him to be in complete isolation" (Winnicott, 1952, p. 222) *and* when ready, to make "a spontaneous movement" (p. 222) which the mother recognizes and responds to "without loss of [the infant's] sense of self" (p. 222). The need to be an isolate intertwined with the need to be recognized continues throughout life as perhaps our most fundamental onto-logical set of needs. Without recognition by another person, we are adrift; we cannot know who we are when in a state of complete isolation (Winnicott, 1967, 1968). And at the same time, we feel a vitally important need to protect the *incommunicado* core of our-selves, which is "sacred" (p. 187).

To be isolated without having to be insulated

On the heels of presenting the idea that each individual is an isolate, Winnicott poses a question for himself and the reader which I think naturally arises from the tension between the need to be found and the need to remain permanently unfound: "The question is: how to be isolated without having to be insulated?" (p. 187). Winnicott's responses to this question are enigmatic. Though he asks (rhetori-cally?), "Shall we stop trying to understand human beings?", I do not think that Winnicott is proposing that we, as analysts, give up our efforts to understand the human condition and the individual lives of our patients. Rather, it seems to me that he is saying that if we were to "stop trying to understand," we might be able to engage with our patients in a different, fuller way:

> The answer might come from mothers who do not commu-nicate with their infants except in so far as they are subjective objects.
>
> (p. 188)

I find it significant that the sentence is structured in the form of "do not communicate … except in so far," as opposed to "communicate only in so far." The structure Winnicott uses forces the reader to live, for a moment, with the idea of not communicating *at all*, before the absolute is modified. Winnicott has returned to using the term "subjective objects," but the term has again taken on a new set of meanings. The term now seems to refer to an object relationship characterized by a *state of being* in which the mother and infant are

44

so closely tied to one another that the mother communicates with her infant (both expressively and receptively) in a way that does not involve "understanding." So a different, fuller way in which the analyst might help the patient (and himself) to be isolated without being insulated involves not communicating with the patient, except in so far as the patient is a subjective object.

Winnicott then moves to a far more mature form of object-relating as he continues to respond to the question, "How to be isolated without being insulated?"

> By the time mothers become objectively perceived their infants have become masters of various techniques for indirect communication, the most obvious of which is the use of language.
>
> (p. 188)

Winnicott, once again, leaves it to the reader to "write" the meaning of the term "indirect communication." As I read/write this sentence, the use of language is "indirect communication" in that verbal symbolization involves words that derive their meaning from a shared set of symbols. This is "indirect" in the sense that the word *house*, for example, has no direct (inherent) connection with a house, nor does the word *green* have any inherent connection with the color green. By contrast (it seems to me), direct communication involves altering the feeling state of another person in a way that is unmediated by symbols, for example, by means of a patient's shouting at the analyst or threatening to commit suicide or to murder the analyst. Screaming and threatening, for example, do not depend on symbolic meaning; they are menacing actions in their own right—they are what they are: imminent destructive activity. Projective identification might be thought of as a form of direct communication in that the "projector" elicits feeling states in the "recipient" by means of actual interpersonal pressure (in concert with an unconscious fantasy of occupying and controlling the recipient from within). As I use the word *unconscious* in the previous sentence, I am reminded of the fact that Winnicott rarely uses the term in this paper, replacing it with words such as *unfound, isolated, incommunicado, not-communicating, silent*, and so on.

In the final sentence of this dense paragraph, written in response to the question, "How to be isolated without being insulated?", Winnicott returns to the idea that in addition to communication with subjective objects and communication with objects objectively perceived, there is a third form of relating and communicating "in which transitional objects and phenomena have a place" (p. 188), a "place" of a different nature from either communicating with subjective objects or with objectively perceived objects. I would add that as one achieves the capacity to experience the object as a separate person, one increasingly communicates what one's feelings *are like* as opposed to what one's feelings *are*—no one can actually communicate his feelings to another person or experience another person's feelings (even in the case of mothers relating to their infants as subjective objects). Consequently, communication holds the potential to be a richly creative experience, an "art" in the most ordinary sense of the word—using facial expressions and gestures and words to bring thoughts and feelings to life. And it is in transitional space that creativity and art are born:

> [One] can talk about the mental mechanisms of the artist but not about the experience of communication in art and religion unless he is willing to peddle in the intermediate area whose ancestor is the infant's transitional object.
>
> (p. 184)

What to do while waiting?

Having made what he views as the "main [theoretical] point" of his paper—the idea that the individual is an isolate, "permanently unknown, in fact unfound"—Winnicott goes on to make, what seems to me, the main clinical points of his paper. He says that a patient and analyst may fail to make progress if they fill the sessions with an "infinitely prolonged" (p. 189) flow of words that serve as a "negation of non-communication" (p. 189). This represents an unconscious effort (in which patient and analyst collude) to use spoken words to drown out the experience of the silent central core of the patient. "[I]n the kind of case I have in mind the analyst had better wait" (p. 189) to interpret, for interpreting would simply add another layer of verbiage. This clinical point addresses analytic work with healthier patients, "the clear-cut neurotic case" (p. 189), though to my mind, the "clear-cut neurotic" aspect of a patient always lives in tension with what Bion (1957) calls "the psychotic part of the personality."

But this type of collusion, though it produces "lack of result" (p. 189), is not the most damaging outcome that may occur in an analysis.

> More dangerous … is the state of affairs in an analysis in which the analyst is permitted by the patient to reach the deepest layers of the analysand's personality because of his position as subjective object, or because of the dependence of the patient in the transference psychosis; here there is danger if the analyst interprets instead of waiting for the patient to creatively discover. It is only here, at the place when the analyst has not changed over from a subjective object to one that is objectively perceived, that psycho-analysis is dangerous, and the danger is one that can be avoided if we know how to behave ourselves. If we wait we become objectively perceived in the patient's own time, but if we fail to behave in a way that is facilitating the patient's analytic process … we suddenly become not-me for the patient, and then we know too much, and we are dangerous because we are too nearly in communication with the central still and silent spot of the patient's ego organization.
>
> (p. 189)

One can hear in this passage echoes of the question Winnicott posed earlier: "Shall we stop trying to understand human beings?" and his response to that question: we might learn from "mothers who do not communicate with their infants except in so far as they are subjective objects." In the passage just quoted, Winnicott holds that it is perhaps our most important responsibility to our patient to recognize the power we possess to violate the patient's sacred core by "suddenly becoming not-me," suddenly "know[ing] too much" in the act of interpreting "instead of waiting for the patient to creatively discover." We "behave ourselves" by "waiting" (as subjective objects) until the patient in his "own time" is ready to experience us as separate objects.

While the considerable differences between Winnicott's theory and technique and those of Melanie Klein are evident throughout this paper, nowhere does Winnicott draw such emphatic lines between his approach and Klein's as he does in the passage just cited (though he does not mention her by name). I infer that he is referring to her analytic technique when he speaks here of "the analyst [who] interprets instead of waiting" and when he warns of "know[ing] too much." Winnicott contrasts this with his own approach to interpretation: "I have always felt that an important function of the interpretation is the establishment of the limits of the analyst's understanding" (p. 189).

Moreover, this paragraph just quoted, for me, is one of Winnicott's most succinct and penetrating commentaries on how he conducts himself as an analyst (not only with severely ill patients, but with all patients as they engage with him as a subjective object). This leaves it to the reader to put into words ("to write") what he, as analyst, does while he waits. We cannot remain silent session after session, week after week, while we are waiting (Winnicott, 1963b), for in my experience as an analyst, and as a consultant to analysts and analysands, such unremitting silence at the juncture in analysis that Winnicott is describing, leads the patient to feel that the analyst has disappeared.

Each analyst, with each of his patients, in each session, must respond to the question, "What do I do while I wait?" And in doing so, the analyst consciously and unconsciously takes direction from the patient.

In what follows, I describe an experience with a patient in which it was essential that I "wait" (as a predominantly subjective object) and not "know too much."

When I entered the waiting room to meet Mr. N for the first time, he was seated, his head and body bent forward, looking at the floor. The patient was a late-middle-aged man with a somewhat disheveled appearance. Even while I introduced myself, Mr. N made no eye contact, nor did he say a word. I had a strong suspicion even before we left the waiting room that the patient was psychotic.

Once in the consulting room, Mr. N kept his gaze to the floor and spoke in a soft, mumbling way that was very difficult to hear. I could not make sense of what I was able hear. I was eventually able to discern the beginning of a sentence: "It's very hard to walk out ..." I guessed he was telling me that it was difficult for him to walk out of the consulting room, perhaps because he did not want to leave, or felt that I was in some way preventing him from leaving, or he felt unable to move his body. It seemed to me that he meant all three and probably many other things as well. In order not to prematurely fill the analytic space with myself as a not-me object, I simply repeated his words to him, "It's very hard to walk out …" He replied to my repetition of his words with a mumbled, "That's right," which led me to smile. I cannot say precisely why his response made me smile, but it may have been that I felt he was telling me in a somewhat humorous way that I had gotten it right.

Mr. N continued to mumble for what seemed like a very long time, during which, without realizing it, I was sitting at the edge of my chair, leaning forward, with my muscles tensed, struggling to make out what he was saying, even if it was only a sentence fragment or a phrase. At some point, perhaps 15 or 20 minutes into the session, I just stopped trying to hear and make sense of what Mr. N was mumbling. I leaned back in my chair and felt the tension drain from my body. It was an enormously freeing feeling, not a feeling of giving up on the analytic work, but a feeling that it was not important that I understand, rather it was important that I not understand and just allow to happen what was going to happen without trying to understand it or change it (or change the patient into someone else).

As we sat together quietly, my mind wandered. I was looking forward to consulting to a new group of analysts with whom I had begun working a few weeks earlier. One of the analysts had missed the meetings after attending only the first. I wondered why. Had I done something to upset her? I liked Mr. N already, but worried that this would be the last time I would see him. I had a memory of working with a schizophrenic patient who refused to say a single word to me and had managed to get me to feel like killing him. I thought of another patient who was admitted to the ER one night when I was moonlighting during my residency. The patient was a bulimic student who had just eaten two full loaves of bread and several broiled chickens. She had stretched her stomach to the point that she developed such extensive gangrene of her stomach walls that an emergency gastrectomy had to be performed before her stomach burst. I did not try to draw one-to-one correspondences between these thoughts and what was happening in the session.

After some time—it was difficult to judge how long—Mr. N began to speak indistinctly again, this time a bit more audibly. He said, "Can you … [inaudible words] me." This time I imagined he was asking me if I could help him, but it also came to mind that he might be asking me if I could kill him. I might have said to another patient, "You're not sure what you want from me," but the use of the words "you" and "me" in the sentence would not have suited this patient in this session because it seems to me, as I look back on it, that by using those personal pronouns, I would be prematurely presenting myself as a not-me object. Also, for Mr. N, my speaking in that way would have conveyed too much of a sense that I was telling him what he was thinking, which would have felt to him, I believe, that I was invading with my thoughts his "central still and silent" core. What's more, that comment would have failed to convey anything of the warmth I felt for Mr. N. I said to him, "So much has happened in such a short time."

The end of the session was approaching. I asked Mr. N, "Should we set up a time to meet again?"

He said, "Yes," using full-voiced clarity for the first time in the session.

Throughout the session, I refrained from asking Mr. N to repeat anything that I was not able to understand because he was telling me in the only way he had of telling me that, paradoxically, it was important that *I be there to not understand*. To put that in other terms, it was important that I allow myself to enter into an experience with the patient in which we communicated in small bits of sentence fragments supplemented by communications in the form of what we each elicited in the other emotionally. For me, as the analyst, this took the form of the reverie experience I have described. I use the term *reverie* to refer to the analyst's waking dreaming in the analytic session. It is a type of receptivity to derivatives of what is occurring at an unconscious level in the analytic relationship (usually in the form of what on the surface seems like one's own meandering thoughts) (Ogden, 1994, 1997).

I view my reverie experience in the session not as a form of withdrawing into myself, but as a form of emotional connection with the patient *and* as a way of talking to myself, a way of thinking about what was happening which helped to establish for the patient and myself my separateness, my ability to think and feel and conduct myself as a person separate from Mr. N. If he were to lose all sense of me as other, he would be the only person in the room, which would have left him feeling utterly alone, utterly adrift. If there is no object, there is no subject. The patient is no one. As I think back on it now, that moment in the session when I stopped trying so hard to hear and understand, and could sit back in my chair, was a moment at which I was accepting the separateness of the patient and me. My leaning back in the way that I did was another way that

I communicated to Mr. N that I was a separate person who could tolerate, and even enjoy, the fact that there was a divide between us, that we were not one person.

The delicate balance of the states of being that I have described constituted my own way of "waiting" with Mr. N during this session in which it was critical that I conduct myself in a way that allowed him to communicate and not communicate, to be understood and not be understood.

Since my way of "waiting," of communicating with the patient predominantly as a subjective object, takes a different form with every patient in every session, I will briefly describe how I work under such circumstances with three other patients. It will be apparent that I have no "formula," no "set of rules," that governs how I conduct myself while I wait with a patient who is so deeply and primitively dependent on me that he or she can tolerate awareness of my separateness only to a very minimal degree. I, as analyst, must, here too create analysis anew with each patient in each session (see Chapter 3 and Chapter 5).

Ms. T, during such a period of analysis, told me with intense shame that she had spent the entire weekend in bed. I said, "It's safe there." The patient continued to spend weekends in bed, but felt less ashamed about it. (I did not say, "You feel safe there," for to have done so would have been to tell the patient what she was feeling, as opposed to simply describing what she was feeling, which, I believe, minimized her sense of my separateness from her. I should emphasize that I would characterize my background state of being with Ms. T at this juncture as "dreamy," unhurried, little concerned with measuring therapeutic progress. And the comments I made carried that sense of profound acceptance of what is.)

Ms. B, at a juncture where I felt it was important that I not know too much, talked about the recent death of her mother. She said, "It's so hard to believe she's not here at all, she's completely gone." I responded by saying, "It is strange, isn't it, that people disappear … while chairs don't." Ms. B smiled. (I introduced a metaphor that unobtrusively added another layer of meaning. And as importantly, there was a feeling of closeness between Ms. B and me as we enjoyed the "soft" sense of amazement and humor in that moment.)

Ms. L, at a juncture in analysis of the sort I am discussing, was feeling exhausted by her child's "incessant demands." The patient was losing weight to the point that her clothes looked baggy on her.

Her child, too, was struggling. I said to her halfway through one of these sessions, "As you talk today, I've been thinking of the yolk of an egg that the chick uses to live off of while it grows in its shell, until that final moment when the egg cracks open and the yolk has been fully consumed." Ms. L was quiet for the remainder of the session. In the sessions that followed, she made no direct reference to my comment, but in her accounts of the way she experienced and responded to her child, there was more genuine tenderness in her voice than I had previously heard. (Here, too, I did not use a sentence structured in terms of "I" and "you"; rather, I simply offered a description, a metaphor, a narrative, an image, the details of which conveyed a bit more than the patient had told me about the way she felt as mother to her child, and it seemed that she was able to use that added layer of meaning in becoming the mother she so desperately wanted to be.)

In sum, in each of these clinical situations, I found myself—without planning what I was going to say or how I was going to say it—describing, as opposed to naming, explaining, or interpreting. The descriptions were not mere repetitions of what the patient had said. They added further meaning with enough "otherness" that there was something new for the patient to make use of, while not being so other, so "not-me," that the patient felt the need to retreat into himself or herself.

Communicating the inexpressible

In the final portion of his paper, the language Winnicott uses to express his ideas regarding communicating and not communicating undergoes significant change. Now completely absent is any use of the term *subjective object*; and in its place are words and sentences that seem to attempt to transcend the limits of language in an effort to express the inexpressible, to attempt to find words and metaphors to convey a sense of the state of being in which we are alive at our core. Winnicott begins the final section:

> I am ... claiming that at the core of the individual there is no communication with the not-me world either way. Here quietude is linked with stillness.
>
> (pp. 189–190)

And he adds a bit later,

> It is here that silence is equated with communication and still-
> ness with movement.
>
> (p. 191)

I find myself straining to "understand" how "silence is equated with communication and stillness with movement." But, of course, when I try to "understand" or paraphrase, the aliveness of the language is lost. The realm of experience toward which Winnicott is gesturing may be one in which silence is a communication (to no one but one-self) of a state of pure being, and stillness is movement at the center of one's turning world.

Winnicott, earlier in the paper, proposed that the central core of the self is formed by means of a split in the psyche in which one part, the false self, "manages" external reality, while the other part becomes engaged in a "communication with subjective objects [that] ... carries all the sense of real" (p. 184). At the very end of the paper, he uses quite different language to state his conception of the origin of the experience of aliveness:

> In healthy development the infant (theoretically) starts off (psy-
> chologically) without life and becomes lively simply because of
> being, in fact, alive. ... [T]his being alive is the early commu-
> nication of a healthy infant with the [healthy] mother-figure,
> and it is as unselfconscious as can be.
>
> (p. 192)

In this passage, there is beauty and life in the writing, in the sound of the words: the infant "becomes lively simply because of being, in fact, alive. ... [B]eing alive is the early communication ... with the mother-figure, and it is as unselfconscious as can be." I cannot recall any other analytic writer using such an ordinary expression—"and it is as unselfconscious as can be"—in such an expressive way. The beauty and ordinariness of the language conveys a sense of wonder and surprise in the ordinary communicating that comes naturally to the mother and the newborn: "To be alive is all" (p. 192).

The penultimate paragraph of the paper contains some of the most powerful, most mystifying, and most significant parts of the paper:

[W]e have to recognize this aspect of health: the non-communicating central self, for ever immune from the reality principle, and for ever silent. Here communication is not non-verbal; it is, like the music of the spheres, absolutely personal. It belongs to being alive. And in health, it is out of this that communication naturally arises.

(p. 192)

"Here communication is not non-verbal": this is the first time in the entire paper that Winnicott introduces the astonishing idea that at the core of the self, communication is neither verbal nor non-verbal. I ask myself, what does that leave if communicating is not done *with* words and is not done *without* words? The question is unanswerable, which is perhaps the true "main theme" of this paper: Winnicott is exploring what we cannot conceive of, much less put into words: the experience at the core of our being.

He continues in the same sentence: "it is like the music of the spheres"—a metaphor unlike any other Winnicott has used in this paper, a metaphor that invokes Pythagoras's fifth-century BC notion of music of perfect harmony, inaudible to human beings, produced by the movement of celestial bodies. Such a metaphor is to be marveled at, and struggled with, but not "understood" or "figured out." "Here"—at the core of our being—communication is unimaginable. And how better to describe that silent communication than with the words: "absolutely personal. It belongs to being alive"?

Concluding comments

Winnicott's paper is a paper of paradox, opposites, and mutually dependent, mutually enriching ideas. The most central of the paradoxes is the idea that communication with subjective objects at the core of the self, while absolutely non-communicating, nonetheless endows every aspect of one's experience with "the sense of real." Most prominent among the mutually dependent conceptions is the composite idea that while it is disaster to be found—more violating of the self than rape—it is at the same time disaster not to be found, not to be recognized. And the most important of the opposites are two opposites of communicating, two very different forms of non-communicating: (1) defensive withdrawal in response to violation of the defenses of the core self; and (2) the state of *incommunicado* isolation that characterizes the healthy core self.

But, to my mind, as original as is the idea that *"each individual is an isolate, permanently non-communicating, permanently unknown, in fact unfound,"* the paper would be less radical in its vision if its trajectory did not carry Winnicott to the place where he arrives at the end of the paper, a place I imagine Winnicott did not anticipate when he commenced writing it. At its close, Winnicott's use of words becomes the language of poetry, for nothing less is required if it is to transcend the limits of language in the process of gesturing toward the inexpressible. The term *subjective object*, though reinvented several times in the course of the paper, drops away completely in the final portion of the essay. So, too, does the term *objectively perceived object*, and even the term *isolate*. Instead, concerning the core self, Winnicott writes, "It is here that silence is equated with communication, stillness with movement." He asks us to try to conceive of the inconceivable: communication that is neither verbal nor nonverbal; "it is, like the music of the spheres, absolutely personal. It belongs to being alive." These words are impossible to paraphrase or explain. They are an expression of the mystery of being that is "absolutely personal" to each of us.

References

Abram, J. (1996). *The Language of Winnicott: A Dictionary of Winnicott's Use of Words*. London: Karnac.

Bion, W. R. (1957). Differentiation of the psychotic from the non-psychotic parts of the personality. In *Second Thoughts*. New York: Aronson, 1967, pp. 93–109.

Ogden, T. H. (1989). On the concept of an autistic-contiguous position. *The International Journal of Psychoanalysis*, 70:127–140.

Ogden, T. H. (1991). Some theoretical comments on personal isolation. *Psychoanalytic Dialogues*, 1:377–390.

Ogden, T. H. (1994). The analytic third—working with intersubjective clinical facts. *The International Journal of Psychoanalysis*, 75:3–120.

Ogden, T. H. (1997). Reverie and interpretation. *The Psychoanalytic Quarterly*, 66:567–595.

Tustin, F. (1984). Autistic shapes. *The International Review of Psycho-Analysis*, 11:279–290.

Winnicott, D. W. (1952). Psychoses and child care. In *Through Paediatrics to Psycho-Analysis*. New York: Basic Books, pp. 219–228.

Winnicott, D. W. (1963a). Communicating and not communicating leading to a study of certain opposites. In *The Maturational Processes and the Facilitating Environment*. New York: International Universities Press, 1965, pp. 179–192.

Winnicott, D. W. (1963b). Two notes on the use of silence. In *Psycho-Analytic Explorations*, edited by C. Winnicott, R. Shepherd, and M. Davis. Cambridge, MA: Harvard University Press, 1989, pp. 81–86.

Winnicott, D. W. (1967). The mirror-role of mother and family in child development. In *Playing and Reality*. New York: Basic Books, pp. 111–118.

Winnicott, D. W. (1968). Communication between infant and mother, and mother and infant, compared and contrasted. In *Babies and Their Mothers*, edited by C. Winnicott, R. Shepherd, and M. Davis. Reading, MA: Addison-Wesley, pp. 89–104.

Winnicott, D. W. (1969). The use of an object and relating through identifications. In *Playing and Reality*. New York: Basic Books, pp. 86–94.

3

HOW I TALK WITH MY PATIENTS[1]

Perhaps the most important clinical questions, and the most difficult ones for me as a practicing psychoanalyst, are those not so much concerned with *what* I say to my patients, as they are with *how* I talk with my patients. In other words, my focus over the years has moved from *what I mean* to *how I mean*. Of course, the two are inseparable, but in this chapter I place emphasis on the latter. I will discuss problems and possibilities spawned by the recognition that we can never know the patient's experience; the impossibility of generalizing about how we talk with patients given that it is incumbent upon the analyst to reinvent psychoanalysis with each patient; the analyst's approach to the patient's fear of psychic change; the way in which the analyst's "off-ness," his misunderstandings and misstatements may foster creative expression on the part of both patient and analyst; and the ways in which describing experience, as opposed to explaining it, better fosters discourse that addresses the unconscious level of what is occurring in the analysis. In the clinical work I present, I describe my own spoken and unspoken thoughts concerning *how* I talk with the patient.

Patient and analyst in every moment of their work together bump up against the fact that the immediacy of their lived experience is incommunicable. No one has described the breach between the minds of human beings as well as William James (1890):

> Each of these minds [in this lecture-hall] keeps its own thoughts to itself. There is no giving or bartering between them. No thought even comes into direct sight of a thought in another personal consciousness than its own. Absolute insulation, irreducible pluralism, is the law … The breaches between such

DOI: 10.4324/9781003228462-3

> thoughts [the thoughts of two different people] are the most absolute breaches in nature.
>
> (p. 226)

Thus, in talking with patients, my own experience is incommunicable; the experience of the patient, inaccessible: I can never know the experience of the patient. Words and physical expression fall far short of communicating the patient's or my own lived experience. Nonetheless, the patient and I may be able to communicate *something like* our lived experiences by re-presenting the experience. This may involve using language that is particular to each of us and to the emotional event that is occurring, for example, by means of metaphor, irony, hyperbole, rhythm, rhyme, wit, slang, syntax, and so on, as well as bodily expression such as shifts in speaking tone, volume, and tempo, and quality of eye contact.

This divide between the patient's subjectivity and my own is not an impediment to be overcome; it is a space in which a dialectic of separateness and intimacy may give rise to creative expression. In the analytic setting, if communicating individual experience were somehow possible, the patient and I would be robbed of the need/ opportunity to creatively imagine the experiences of the other. Paradoxically, the parts that are missing, the parts left out of our communications open a space in which we may be able, in some way, to bridge the gap between ourselves and others. The patient's experience of *being creative* in the act of communicating is an essential part of the process of his "dreaming himself more fully into existence" (Ogden, 2004, p. 858), coming into being in a way that is uniquely his own.

The impossibility of knowing the experience of another person has important implications for the way I talk with my patients. For instance, I try not to tell a patient what he or she is thinking and feeling for the simple reason that I cannot know this; instead, I try to limit myself to saying only what *I* think and feel. It is important to add that this is not a rigid rule I impose upon myself. Rather, as with almost everything having to do with talking with patients, how I talk to a patient, in every instance, hinges upon what is happening between this particular patient and me at this particular moment.

When I do speak with a patient about what I sense is happening emotionally in the session, I might say something like: "While you were talking [or during the silence], this room felt like a very empty place [or peaceful place, or confusing place, and so on]." In phrasing things in this way, I leave open the question of who is feeling the emptiness (or other feelings). Was it the patient, or I, or something the two of us have unconsciously created together (the "analytic field" [Civitarese, 2008, 2016; Ferro, 2005, 2011] or the "analytic third" [Ogden 1994])? Almost always, it is all three—the patient and I as separate individuals, and our unconscious co-creations.

I have found that asking a patient questions such as, "Why have you been so silent today?" or "Why did you decide to skip yesterday's session?" invite the patient to move to the surface level of his experience, to think and speak with me in conscious, logical, sequential, chronological, cause-and-effect (secondary process) modes of thinking. So, when I find myself asking questions that invite secondary process thinking on the part of either the patient or me, I pause to wonder, what is it about the unconscious aspect of what is occurring that is frightening me?

The analyst's feeling of certainty is often tied to the idea that there exists a proper "analytic technique" derived from ideas passed down from one generation of analysts to the next (which may be codified by particular "schools" of analytic thinking). By contrast, I think of "analytic style" as one's own personal creation that is loosely based on existing principles of analytic practice, but more importantly is a living process that has its origins in the personality and experience of the analyst (Ogden, 2007). It is essential that we not incorporate into our practice of analysis a now out-moded view that the patient's antagonism to the analytic process frequently represents an effort to kill the analysis or kill the analyst. Such a viewpoint forecloses the analyst's capacity to reflect upon the transference–countertransference dimensions of the patient's "opposition" to analytic work. Winnicott (1963) focuses on a type of fear of analytic work that arises from the patient's need to protect himself from "being found before being there [before developing an identity] to be found" (p. 190). Schafer (1980, 1983a, 1983b) has written extensively about the dangers of interpreting the patient's resistance and the need for holding an "affirmative attitude" (p. 12), an approach that entails a compassionate, understanding response to the patient's unconscious reasons for fighting psychic change. In my experience, a patient's "unwillingness" or "inability" to do analytic work almost always reflects the transference–countertransference equivalent of the method he developed in infancy and childhood to protect his sanity and his very life, a method I view with respect and even admiration.

But when carried over into adulthood, the psychic techniques that helped the patient preserve his sanity and his life in infancy and childhood may become severely limiting of his capacity to learn from experience, to engage in mature relationships with both internal and external objects, to become himself in as full a way as he might. The patient's experience of these limitations, and the psychic pain associated with them, are almost always the underlying forces that lead the patient to seek out help from analysis.

If an analysis has progressed to any significant degree, differences can be felt by both the patient and me between the present situation and what we imagine to be the patient's childhood experience. First, the patient felt alone in infancy and childhood with regard to the problems he was facing—a terrifying feeling that he was trapped with people with whom genuine communication and real change were impossible (and the patient and analyst experience something like this state of affairs in the transference–countertransference relationship). But the patient may also be able to sense that in some way he is no longer as utterly alone as he once was. Secondly, the patient is no longer a child, and is in possession of psychic capacities for handling the threat to his sanity and his life that he did not have available to him as a child. These felt differences have provided an important underpinning of hope in the analyses I have conducted.

In my experience, certainty may also impinge upon the analytic process when patient and/or analyst holds the parents exclusively responsible for the patient's current emotional problems. While it may seem true to the patient and me that he was severely neglected, disparaged, sexually or violently abused by his parents, I have come to realize that it is incumbent upon me not to introduce or join the patient in "parent-blaming." By participating in this oversimplification, I collude in robbing the patient of the opportunity to experience his life in a more complex, and perhaps more humane way, which may come to include an understanding of the patient's rational and irrational sense of responsibility for the problems he experienced in childhood. The patient's painful and guilt-ridden sense of responsibility for the destructiveness of what occurred in his childhood may be kept from view by the firm belief on his part (and mine) that he was a passive victim of parental neglect or abuse.

A parent-blaming approach on the part of the analyst may so oversimplify the patient's experience of—or *inability* to experience (Winnicott, 1974 [1971])—what occurred, that genuine integration of childhood experiences in all of their complexity is rendered all the more difficult. An experience with a patient with whom I worked in analysis many years ago comes to mind in this connection. As a child, he had been brutally beaten by his father. Of this I had not the slightest doubt. But it was only after a great deal of analytic work had been done that the patient became able to tell me a secret that felt unimaginably shameful to him: the "fact" that he had repeatedly provoked his father into anger to the point that he beat the patient. Only after the patient could entrust me and himself with this memory, or perhaps it was a fantasy (it made no difference in the analysis), could he come to understand that provoking his father, if indeed he did so, could only have been an unconscious effort on his part to create the illusion that he had some control over his father's terrifying anger and violence. I said to the patient in response to his entrusting me with his secret, "If you provoked your father in the way you say you did, it was no doubt the best thing you could have done under the circumstances. I believe it saved your life to have some tiny sliver of a sense of control under those circumstances." If I had been judgmental from the outset of the analysis in the form of participating in parent-blaming, I think that the patient would have had much greater difficulty gaining access to his unconscious (or not yet experienced) unspeakably "shameful" memory/fantasy.

I have also found that a shift from *explaining* to *describing* facilitates the analytic process by freeing both patient and me of the need to understand. "Merely" describing, as opposed to "discovering causes" for what is happening, reflects my sense of humility in the face of all that is "humanly understandable or humanly unununderstandable" (Jarrell, 1955, p. 62) in the lives of my patients and in the life of the analysis.

An example of describing instead of explaining took place in an initial analytic meeting (which I mentioned above, p. 23). Earlier in my development as an analyst, if a patient in an initial meeting were to begin by telling me that she felt terrified by coming to see me, I might have asked, "What terrifies you?" or "Why are you terrified?" More recently, when a patient began by telling me she was terrified to come to see me, I said, "Of course you are." My response was what I think of as a description-in-action, that is, a description of my acceptance of her exactly as she is, that is, terrified of me, and a way of welcoming her fantasies instead of trying to dispel them by coming up with conscious, "logical" (secondary process) reasons for them or by means of reassurance. The patient was visibly surprised by what I said, which may have had something to do with her response, which surprised me: "I'm not sure I'm in the right office, but I'll stay for a while." Her response suggested that I was not what she expected, but she was now more curious than terrified, and was going "to stay for a while" to find out more about what, and with whom, she was getting herself involved.

A second example of describing rather than explaining occurred in a session several years into Mr. M's analysis. The patient said that he had begun to tell his wife a dream he had had in which their son was dead. Before he could go into further detail, she said, "Stop, I don't want to hear any more." I said to Mr. M, "Good for her."

When I spontaneously said, "Good for her," I had in mind the idea (or perhaps more accurately, I felt) that just as the patient is all of the figures in his dreams, he is also all of the figures in his accounts of his daily life. In his story about telling his wife the dream, I viewed the patient as not only himself, but also his (interrupting) wife. I believe that the patient experienced my saying, "Good for her," as my recognizing and valuing *his act of interrupting himself*. The patient paused after I made this comment, and then said he felt relieved when she interrupted him. It seemed to me that his response was a reflection of his recognizing he had come some way in the course of the analysis in becoming able to interrupt himself when he felt the impulse to evacuate his unbearable feelings "into" others.

In neither of these examples did I explain something to the patient; instead, I offered succinct descriptions of feeling states: "Of course you are" (what you are feeling now seems only natural) and "Good for her" (your stopping yourself from evacuating feeling is an achievement to be recognized).

A woman not yet a girl

Ms. Y and I had spoken briefly by phone when she called to set up an appointment. When I opened the door to the waiting room, I was surprised to see a woman who I guessed was in her early twenties, but could have been much older or much younger. She was dressed in the accoutrements of the hippie, flower-child era. She wore an ankle-length dress that looked as if she had purchased it at a second-hand clothing store. The dress was large enough to hide almost all curvature of her body. Beaded necklaces of an assortment of lengths and colors were draped from her neck in a way that added a further layer of distraction from the shape of her body.

Upon my introducing myself as Dr. Ogden, the patient responded not in words, but by staring deeply into my eyes in the way (I imagined) a shabby medium or psychic might meet the eyes of a prospective customer. Ms. Y slowly lifted herself from the waiting room chair while maintaining eye contact with me. I said, "Please come in," gesturing toward the open door to the hallway, but by the slightest forward tilt of her head, she indicated that I should lead the way. I glanced back when I heard the patient closing the door to the waiting room, but once we were walking in the carpeted hallway between the waiting room and the consulting room, I could no longer hear her footfalls behind me. An image of Orpheus and Eurydice's journey back from the underworld went through my mind as I decided not to turn to see if she was following. On reaching the consulting room, I opened the door and stepped aside to allow Ms. Y to enter the room ahead of me. She looked back at me to ask wordlessly where she should sit, or perhaps lie on the couch. Motioning to the armchair across the room, I said, "Please have a seat."

I felt as if I were an actor in a film in which I was being asked to improvise a scene of doctor and patient sitting down to begin the first analytic session. There was an otherworldly quality that this patient seemed to work hard to sustain, but I was left with a feeling of deep sadness for this actress who seemed to be condemned to endlessly play a role in the same drama and to try to conscript people into playing the other characters in the play. (I spoke only two or three brief sentences and the patient said nothing in words during the complex scene that was evolving.)

I sat down in my chair which is positioned behind the couch and directly facing the patient's armchair. After getting settled, I looked over at Ms. Y in a way that invited her to begin. There then followed a silence sufficiently long for me to study her face. She wore no makeup and while there was no trace of dirt on her face, I imagined that she had not bathed for some time, as if she were a gypsy. While she had facial features that I found attractive, she seemed utterly devoid of male or female sexuality. She was, in that sense, lifeless and consequently a bit of a cipher.

It became apparent after the silence went on for some time that Ms. Y was not gathering her thoughts; she was waiting for me to begin. I did not allow this silence to turn into a power struggle or a psychic hole into which the patient might fall. (I very rarely let a silence at the beginning of an initial analytic session go on for more than half a minute or so.) I said, "It feels to me as if our meeting began some time ago."

"Please tell me what you mean," Ms. Y said in a way that seemed to turn the tables, making me the patient and her the analyst.

I said, rather uncomfortably, "I feel as if I've met several versions of you: while we spoke on the phone, when we met in the waiting room, and while we've been sitting here in this room."

She asked, "What's surprising about that?" But before I had a chance to respond, she added, "I suppose I'm odd."

I looked at her quizzically.

"I guess I try to be unconventional. You're not the first one to find me strange."

"'Strange' isn't a word I use very much. I don't find that being judgmental helps anyone very much."

She said, "That sounds very good, but … I've lost track of what we were talking about." Her sardonic comment about the stereo-typic nature of my response—"That sounds very good"—stung me by its accuracy.

"We're talking about how you sometimes lose track of yourself."

She said with tears welling in her eyes, "I suppose. I really don't know. I don't get what I'm supposed to be doing here."

"There is no *supposed to*." As I listened to myself say this, I felt as if I was not being a real analyst and was once again just playing the role of an analyst. I did not feel like myself, which was a very disturbing feeling. I felt genuinely confused about what I was doing in this room with this patient. Once I began to regain my bearings, it occurred to me that Ms. Y not only did not know why she was sitting in this room with me, she did not know who the woman in the performance was, or whether that woman was still a girl clothed in a costume that belonged more to her mother's generation than her own.

Ms. Y said, "I'm not good at school. I never have been. I say I'm bored, but I just don't get the point of what they're doing there. I'm reading a fantasy book now. You wouldn't like it. My parents hate it. They try to get me to read their books, but they bore me to death. High literature."

I said, "And you're low literature?"

"I guess. Forget it. It's not worth talking about."

"You're not?"

"No, I'm not."

Throughout this part of the meeting, I was aware that I was not asking questions about who Ms. Y was, I was describing what she was saying from a perspective that was surprising to her and began to capture her imagination, for instance, by recasting her statement, "I've lost track of what we're talking about" to "We're talking about how you sometimes lose track of yourself."

I liked Ms. Y. I felt at this point in the session that she had some of the trappings of a woman, but she was psychically a girl who was playing dress–up. Her chronological age was immaterial. It seemed to me that she was not entirely a "no one," "a missing soul"; I felt that there was a bit of someone there hiding in the costume, and a bit of someone who had not yet become herself in any substantial way. I could not know her experience, but I could have some sense of my experience of being with her. Part of what I had to work with consciously was a set of feelings of sadness for her along with discomfort with the feeling I was playing a role in her imprisoning theater, a theater in which she survived, as opposed to lived. At the very edge of my conscious awareness was my curiosity about my feeling I was Orpheus leading Eurydice, trying not to look back.

The patient startled me from my half-dreaming state when she said, "I don't know why I'm here."

I said, "How could you?" I did not respond with statements such as, "Something must have caused you to go to the trouble of coming to see me" or even, "I think you're here because you feel you need help with something." I did not want to push her to come up with conscious reasons or explanations for her behavior, which would serve only as distractions from the unconscious dimension of what was happening.

There was then a long silence. I averted my gaze, which I thought would allow Ms. Y an opportunity to either study my face or to avert her gaze, if she chose to. I could see in the periphery of my vision that she was looking at me in a way that conveyed a sense that she did not know what to make of me. She seemed to me to be like a feral animal, a scavenger without a home. The thought went through my mind, "If she is homeless, what am I going to do with her?"

"Are you afraid of me?" she asked.

I said, "No, I'm not."

"How sweet," she said.

I felt as if I had been slapped across the face—I was being shown the emotional violence Ms. Y was capable of. In the scene being played out, I was in the role of a child whose affection and wish to be liked were met with derision. I also felt that there was some jus-tification for her derisive comment, "How sweet," in that it was not entirely true that I was not frightened of her.

I said, "You can be tough when you need to be."

"I always need to be. I told you I'm strange."

I said, "I'm strange too."

"What do you mean?" she said, sounding more interested than she had previously let herself be.

"Just look at this place. It's in the basement of a house. I spend most of my waking hours here. You have to be strange to do that."

"I guess. Your desk is pretty neat, but I noticed when I came in that there are shreds of paper on the floor that look like they're from one of those wire-bound notebooks that school kids use. To tell you the truth, I thought that was strange, but I liked it. And you're old. That's always a little creepy to me. Sorry if I've insulted you."

"Why shouldn't you take a look at me and at the things in my office that may tell you something about who you're taking a chance on?"

She said, "You've been looking at me, trying to figure me out."

"I'd rather say that I'm trying to get to know you."

She said, "You know already, don't you?"

"So I'm a mind reader," I said.

"I've known mind readers. Really."

I said, "I don't doubt it. I know you're not here to have your mind read, but you may be here to learn how to read your own mind."

"That's a good one. Do they teach you that at shrink school?"

I gave no reply because I did not want to engage with her in that way, which I felt would only distract us from forming a more real form of relatedness. Also, I silently agreed with her that my com-ment sounded canned. I asked myself why I was talking in such a stilted manner with her, a manner that did not sound to me like myself.

After a pause of half a minute or so, she said, "I'm sorry. I'm at it again, aren't I?"

"Could be."

"My mother can read minds."

"Really."

"Not exactly. She's in my head all the time telling me what's wrong with what I'm doing. Not exactly telling. Yelling. I can't get her out of my head."

I was now better able to put into words for myself my sense that Ms. Y was showing me in the way she dressed that she and her mother were one person, the same age, the same style of dressing, the same way of examining, the same way of thinking, the same way of talking, the same way of savaging. But, at the same time, her mother was other to her. The patient was very confused about this, as was I. She felt that her mother was in *her* head, but her head was still *not hers* at this point, which led her to feel afraid of losing herself entirely to the mother-in-her-head. These thoughts about what might be going on were by no means conclusions or explanations; they were impressions, possibilities, wonderings, feelings, descriptions (primarily of shame and loss of my ordinary sense of connection with myself). I did not ask the patient questions about the voice in her head because I was again concerned that questions of that sort would elicit conscious-level (secondary process) responses, which would steer us to the surface, away from the more primitive, undifferentiated aspects of the experience that was occurring in this moment.

I said, "Sounds like a nightmare you can't wake up from."

"She's telling me that I can't trust you."

"I'm not surprised."

"You're not afraid of her?"

"No, I'm not." I did not ask her, "Why should I be?" because, again, I was not after explanations, I was after description. At this point in the session something had changed: I was being truthful when I said that I was not afraid either of the patient or of her mother-in-her-head.

"You should be."

"Really."

"I'm teasing you." She was not only teasing me, she was flirting with me in a lovely way, in a way that reflected some of the ways she had a sense of self that she did not seem to feel was fully in her mother's possession. Her flirting did not feel perverse or theatrical; it felt to me to be a genuine expression of her female way of liking me. There was now a sparkle in her eyes that stood in marked contrast to the pseudo-hypnotizing stare with which she met me in the waiting room.

As the end of the session drew near, I asked Ms. Y if she would like to meet again.

She replied, "Are you going to be the same then as you are now?"

I said, "Yes and no. I expect you'll recognize me as the same person you met today, but I also expect something different will happen in our meeting, which may mean you'll have to get to know me again next time, and I'll have to get to know you again." I felt that I was being verbose and again falling into formulaic speech.

"Then I'll have to call you to let you know."

Ms. Y called a week later saying, "I'd like to meet with you one more time, if that's all right with you."

I said it was all right with me.

We continued to meet on a "one-time-only" basis for about two months before Ms. Y asked to meet regularly. We slowly increased the frequency of meetings to four sessions per week as the patient came to experience me less and less as someone who wished to take over her mind or join her in theatrical performances. However, such suspicions were by no means absent from the transference, any more than feelings that I was only an "imitation analyst" were absent from the countertransference.

In this account of an analytic session, I am describing what I noticed as opposed to collecting clues with which to decipher, figure out, or arrive at an interpretation. My questions to myself were not directed at finding out "Why?" or "How come?" or "What is the cause of the patient's auditory hallucinations?" Instead, I was interested in what it *feels like* to be inhabited in the way this patient was and in the strange and disturbing way in which I was talking with this patient. My observations, impressions, and reveries were not in search of explanations for what was occurring; rather, they were elements I could make use of in my efforts to describe for the patient and myself who the patient was and who I was (at the ever-changing present moment of the session).

The reader will have noticed that I did not ask the patient to help me understand her experience. For example, I did not ask her to "fill in" references she made to particular experiences, such as the sound of her mother-in-her-head yelling critical comments at her. And I did not try to explain myself to the patient, and instead spoke to her in a way that I hoped would elicit in her a tolerable level of anxiety mixed with curiosity (for instance, when I said, "I'm strange too"). I should also say that my failures to speak naturally with the patient were not simply "mistakes"; they were productive expressions of my own loss of connection with myself that mirrored, but did not replicate, the patient's experience of losing track of who she was.

And most of the time I did not attempt to help Ms. Y "understand" what I was saying. My comments were often of the sort: "Really" or "I'm not surprised" or "No, I'm not [afraid]." I sometimes tried to describe (to offer metaphors for) what I imagined the patient was experiencing, for example, when I said, "Sounds like a nightmare you can't wake up from." It was particularly important to include "sounds like" in talking with this patient whose mind was already occupied by (what felt to her to be) two people.

These aspects of the way I spoke with this patient reflect a strong feeling on my part that we all speak with a simultaneous wish to be understood and to be misunderstood, and that we listen to others both with the desire to understand and to misunderstand. The latter—the wish to misunderstand and be misunderstood—only in part reflects a desire not to be known, a desire to maintain an aspect of self that stands in necessary isolation (as described by Winnicott, 1963). In my experience, the patient's wish *to be misunderstood* often strives for more in the way of coming into her own in her own way than does *the wish to be understood*. The wish to be understood inherently carries a wish for closure, a wish to be recognized for who one is at present. By contrast, I find that the patient's wish to be misunderstood involves a wish to dream herself up (as opposed to being seen by the analyst). Respecting the patient's need for self-discovery places a demand on me not to "know too much" (Winnicott 1963, p. 189). Misunderstandings put the patient and me in a position to make use of the "off-ness" of my understanding in an effort to create renderings of her experience that neither she nor I could have anticipated—"it's not *that*, it's more like *this*"—a *this* that could not have been conceived of (dreamt up) without the particular "off-ness" of the understanding. I am reminded here of

James Grotstein's description (in a conversation we had more than 25 years ago) of a moment in his analysis with Bion. In response to one of Bion's interpretations, Grotstein said, "I understand." Bion impatiently responded, "Please try not to understand. If you must, meta-stand, para-stand, circum-stand, but *please* try not to understand" (Grotstein, personal communication, 2008). Understanding, from this perspective, is a rather passive mental activity compared with the act of misunderstanding and doing something with the "off-ness" of the understanding. The work of understanding carries the danger of "killing" an experience that was once alive in an analytic session. Once an experience has been "figured out," it is dead. Once a person is "understood," he is no longer interesting, no longer a living, unfolding, mysterious person.

Note

1   I am grateful to the members of the "Thursday Seminar" for helping me develop some of the clinical thinking I have presented in this chapter.

References

Civitarese, G. (2008). *The Intimate Room: Theory and Technique of the Analytic Field*. London: Routledge.

Civitarese, G. (2016). *Truth and the Unconscious in Psychoanalysis*. London: Routledge.

Ferro, A. (2005). *Seeds of Illness, Seeds of Recovery: The Genesis of Suffering and the Role of Psychoanalysis*. London: Routledge.

Ferro, A. (2011). *Avoiding Emotions, Living Emotions*. London: Routledge.

James, W. (1890). Stream of thought. In *The Principles of Psychology, Vol. 1*. New York: Dover Publications, pp. 224–290.

Jarrell, R. (1955). To the Laodiceans. In *Poetry and the Age*. New York: Vintage, pp. 34–62.

Ogden, T. H. (1994). The analytic third—working with intersubjective clinical facts. *The International Journal of Psychoanalysis*, 75:3–19.

Ogden, T. H. (2004). This art of psychoanalysis: Dreaming undreamt dreams and interrupted cries. *The International Journal of Psychoanalysis*, 85:857–877.

Ogden, T. H. (2007). Elements of analytic style: Bion's clinical seminars. *The International Journal of Psychoanalysis*, 88:1185–1200.

Schafer, R. (1980). Narration in the psychoanalytic dialogue. *Critical Inquiry*, 7:29–53.

Schafer, R. (1983a). *The Analytic Attitude.* New York: Basic Books.

Schafer, R. (1983b). Resisting and empathizing. In *The Analytic Attitude.* New York: Basic Books, pp. 66–81.

Winnicott, D. W. (1963). Communicating and not communicating leading to a study of certain opposites. In *The Maturational Processes and the Facilitating Environment.* New York: International Univ. Press, pp. 179–192.

Winnicott, D. W. (1974) [1971]. Fear of breakdown. In *Psychoanalytic Explorations*, edited by C. Winnicott, R. Shepherd, and M. Davis. Cambridge, MA: Harvard Univ. Press, 1989, pp. 87–95.

4

DESTRUCTION RECONCEIVED

On Winnicott's "The use of an object and relating through identifications"

"The use of an object and relating through identifications" is perhaps Winnicott's most difficult paper and most certainly one of his most important. There is a sad story associated with Winnicott's initial presentation of this paper to the New York Psychoanalytic Institute on the evening of November 12, 1968. To Winnicott's disappointment, the paper received a puzzled and skeptical response. Milrod, in the official minutes of the meeting, wrote: "In a charming and whimsical fashion Dr. Winnicott responded by saying his concept had been torn to pieces and that he would be happy to give it up" (Rodman, 2003, p. 328). Shortly after the meeting, Winnicott suffered a heart attack. A reworked version of the paper presented in New York was published the following year in the *International Journal of Psychoanalysis* (Winnicott, 1969a), and a slightly revised version of that paper was published posthumously in *Playing and Reality* (1971). Winnicott is said to have been "still revising the paper for publication in *Playing and Reality* on the day of his death, January 25, 1971" (Samuels, 2001, p. 38). I will be discussing the 1971 version of the paper.

So much is merely suggested in this paper that one must not only read it, one must also participate in writing it. The ideas I develop in this chapter represent my own reading and writing of Winnicott's paper—what I make *of* it, and more importantly, what I make *with* it.

DOI: 10.4324/9781003228462-4

"The subject of this paper"

Winnicott, in the opening paragraphs of the paper, speaks in an intimate, conversational way that sets the tone for the rest of the paper:

> It appalls me to think how much deep change I have prevented or delayed in patients *in a certain classification category* by my personal need to interpret. If only we can wait, the patient arrives at understanding creatively and with immense joy, and I now enjoy this joy more than I used to enjoy the sense of having been clever. I think I interpret mainly to let the patient know the limits of my understanding. The principle is that it is the patient and only the patient who has the answers.
>
> (pp. 86–87, original emphasis)

While this passage strikes a chord of truth in me, I wonder what Winnicott has in mind when he says, "I interpret mainly to let the patient know the limits of my understanding." He leaves the reader free to develop his or her own "answers" to this question (as he tries to do with his patients). As we will see, Winnicott makes use of the reader's experience of reading this paper to *show* rather than *tell* the reader what he has in mind, for much of what he has in mind cannot be told or explained, it has to be experienced.

Winnicott immediately follows this statement about not interpreting with a statement about the importance of interpreting:

> By contrast with this comes the interpretative work that the analyst must do, which distinguishes analysis from self-analysis. The interpreting by the analyst, if it is to have effect, must be related to the patient's ability *to place the analyst outside the area of subjective phenomena.* What is then involved is the patient's ability to use the analyst, which is the subject of this paper.
>
> (p. 87, original emphasis)

Winnicott, in consecutive paragraphs, presents two *seemingly* contradictory ideas: one must not give in to a "need to interpret" *and* there is "the interpretative work that the analyst must do." Winnicott does not explain the relationship between these ideas, but he offers some guidance when he says, "The interpreting by the analyst, if it is to have effect, must be related to the patient's ability *to place the analyst outside the area of subjective phenomena.*" Interpreting, if it is to "have effect" (if it is to have consequences in the *real* world) must be done only after the patient has developed the capacity to "*to place the analyst outside the area of subjective phenomena.*" Winnicott does not expand on what this sentence means, but says it is "the subject of this paper." Interestingly, later in the paper, Winnicott returns, only in a single brief allusion, to these critically important ideas concerning the analyst's use (or refraining from use) of interpretation.

At this juncture in the paper, the reader is left hanging, not quite understanding what Winnicott has in mind regarding the place of interpretation in analysis, much less how he arrived at his ideas.

A theoretical statement

In the second section of the paper—the "sections" are not named or numbered, but I view the paper as divided into four parts thematically—Winnicott clarifies the difference between the two types of relatedness to objects with which he is concerned in this paper: object–relating and object–usage.

> When I speak of the use of an object, … I take object-relating for granted, and add new features that involve the nature and the behaviour of the object. For instance, *the object, if it is to be used, must necessarily be real in the sense of being part of shared reality, not a bundle of projections.*
>
> (p. 88, my emphasis)

Here, Winnicott reverses the conventional terminology of psychoanalysis by using the term "object-relating" (usually used to refer to mature, whole–object relatedness) to refer to the more primitive (narcissistic) form of object relationship in which the object is "a bundle of projections," an extension of the self; and he uses the term "use of an object" (usually associated with exploitation of another person) to refer to mature object-relatedness in which the subject lives in the outside world of "shared reality," and experiences objects as genuinely external to himself. This reversal causes the reader to loosen his grip on what he thought he knew and to open himself to not knowing.

Winnicott concludes his theoretical statement with a story:

> ..., two babies are feeding at the breast. One is feeding on the self, since the breast and the baby have not yet become (for the baby) separate phenomena. The other is feeding from an other-than-me source, or an object that can be given cavalier treatment without effect on the baby unless it retaliates. Mothers, like analysts, can be good or not good enough; some can and some cannot carry the baby over from relating to usage.
>
> (p. 89)

There are two pieces of "unfinished business" in these sentences that foreshadow the heart of the paper, which is contained in the succeeding section. One is the idea that the other-than-me source "can be given cavalier treatment" by the baby. The other is the ominous qualifying phrase added to "cavalier treatment": "unless it retaliates." Once again, meanings are suggested, but only suggested.

A revolutionary set of ideas

Having defined his terms, Winnicott begins this third and most radical portion of the paper in a surprising way:

> I am now ready to go straight to the statement of my thesis. It seems I am afraid to get there, as I fear that once the thesis is stated the purpose of my communication is at an end, because it is so very simple.
>
> (p. 89)

This way of addressing the reader is unique to Winnicott. No other psychoanalyst writes this way. Here, I believe, Winnicott is showing us *what it feels like* to use objects. He is "ready" to state the main theme of the paper, but finds himself afraid to do so because once he states it to the reader, it falls into the hands of other people (the reader), people who are real, and because they are real and separate people with minds of their own, they are free to do what they will with his ideas, regardless of what he might wish them to do. This is the "thesis" of Winnicott's paper brought to life for the reader in the experience of reading.

His main theme is not at all simple:

> To use an object the subject must have developed a *capacity* to
> use objects. This is part of the change to the reality principle.
> (p. 89, original emphasis)

The first of these two sentences may seem absurdly self-evident:
"To use an object the subject must have developed a *capacity* to
use objects." And yet, what Winnicott is referring to is anything
but self-evident. In fact, this may be the first time any analyst has
explored *the process of developing a capacity to use objects* ("it may not
even have been specifically studied [before]," p. 86). Winnicott suggests in the second of these sentences that his conception of the
process of developing that capacity alters our conception of how the
individual develops the ability to face the real world (how the reality
principle becomes a dimension of human consciousness).

In fleshing out this "main theme," Winnicott begins by saying
that the movement from object-relating to use of an object is an
inborn maturational process that depends on real people ("a facilitating environment," p. 89) for its successful development.

At this point, Winnicott makes a striking statement about the
implications of his "main theme":

> In the sequence [under discussion] one can say that first there is
> object-relating, then in the end there is object-use; in between,
> however, is the most difficult thing, perhaps, in human devel-
> opment; or the most irksome of all the early failures that come
> for mending. This thing that there is in between relating and
> use is the subject's placing of the object outside the area of the
> subject's omnipotent control; that is, the subject's perception
> of the object as an external phenomenon, not as a projective
> entity, in fact recognition of it as an entity in its own right.
> (p. 89)

The stage has now been set for what I find to be the three most
difficult, most enigmatic, and most richly evocative paragraphs in
the paper. These paragraphs are also some of the most unusual in
the analytic literature in terms of their literary form: an imaginary
"conversation" between a preverbal infant and his mother.

The first sentence of these three paragraphs throws down the gauntlet:

> This change (from relating to usage) means that the subject destroys the object.
>
> (p. 89)

Winnicott anticipates objection to this statement by "an armchair philosopher" who holds that "if the object is external, the object will be destroyed by the subject" (pp. 89–90). In other words, if the external object is destroyed by the subject, there can be no such thing as an external object.

Winnicott replies by saying that if the armchair philosopher were to "sit on the floor with his patient" (live an analytic experience with his patient), "he will find that there is an intermediate position":

> ..., after "subject relates to object" comes "subject destroys object" (as it becomes external).
>
> (p. 90)

I am stopped in my tracks by these words. I genuinely do not know what it means for the subject to destroy the object as it becomes external. (I am experiencing here something that only very gradually becomes clear to me, as I read and re-read this paper: the word "destroy" is being re-made in these sentences. It has a meaning no one has ever before given it, and I am only beginning, at this point in the paper, to learn something of what that word means.)

The sentence ends with the words:

> and then [after "subject destroys object"] may come "*object survives* destruction by the subject."
>
> (p. 90, original emphasis)

Winnicott is in effect saying that to move from relating to an object as "a bundle of projections" to relating to an object as a separate person, the subject must destroy the object. I wonder, is Winnicott talking about the fantasy of destroying the object or the subject's *really* destroying the object as a separate entity? And what would

77

it mean to *actually* destroy the external object? If the destruction is simply a fantasy, how is this different from the projections entailed in object-relating? And what does it mean for the object to "survive" if the destruction is the real destruction of the external object, not a fantasied destruction?

It is here that the paper comes most electrifyingly alive:

> A new feature thus arrives in the theory of object-relating [as it evolves into object-usage]. The subject says to the object: "I destroyed you," and the object is there to receive the communication. From now on the subject says: "Hullo object!" "I destroyed you." "I love you." "You have value for me because of your survival of my destruction of you." "While I am loving you I am all the time destroying you in (unconscious) *fantasy*."
>
> (p. 90, original emphasis)

For decades, I have read the words "'Hullo object!' 'I destroyed you.' 'I love you.' 'You have value for me because of your survival of my destruction of you'" as the infant's experience of destroying (renouncing his dependence upon) the *omnipotent internal object mother* (see Ogden, 1983, 1986). I thought that the renunciation (fantasied destruction) of the internal object mother cleared the way for the infant's emerging capacity to experience the realness of the external object mother.

This reading of the "destruction" of the object is at odds with the way I now understand what is occurring when "subject destroys object." It seems to me now that my earlier understanding of the destruction of the object did not include the key element of Winnicott's conception of "subject destroys object": it is the *real* external object (*not* an internal object) that is destroyed in the developmental process of moving from object-relating to object-usage. My misreading, as I see it now, resulted from my inability to understand what it meant for the real external object, a real person, to be destroyed.

After the infant "says" to his mother, "'I destroyed you,' and the object is there to receive the communication," what the infant says to his mother is put in an unforgettable way: "From now on the subject says: 'Hullo object!'"—how better to create in words the relief and the joy in the greeting the infant gives his mother who

78

has survived and whom he loves (and by whom he feels loved) in a way he never before experienced because it can only be experienced with a mother who is a person separate from him? The exclamation point is an important stage direction here.

The infant then proudly and jubilantly re-exclaims his achievement, this time with more confidence and pride: "'I destroyed you.' 'I love you.' 'You have value for me because of your survival of my destruction of you.'"

Each time I read these exuberant words, I remember vividly one of my own children—who must have been about six months old—sitting in his high chair like a king with his food tray in front of him. I recall the wide grin on his face as he looked at me straight in the eyes and picked up the small bit of a frankfurter that I had placed on the tray, and I remember his exhilaration as he used his full muscle strength to hurl it to the ground as he screamed with delight. I would pick up the frankfurter and place it back on the tray, never losing eye contact with him, and he would grin, hurl, and jubilantly scream with joy again as he threw it to the ground again. (He had begun playing a kindred game, the peek-a-boo game, a few months earlier, but that game lacked the jubilance of the dropping game.)

But this happy picture is not the picture of the "intermediate position" (p. 90) between object-relating and use of an object. Rather, it is a picture of the great relief and joy felt by the infant on finding that his primary objects are sturdy and can be treated thoughtlessly, dismissively, casually, insouciantly, playfully, scornfully, ragefully, cavalierly, and all the while the object can be counted on to survive. "The subject can now *use* the object that has survived" (p. 90, original emphasis). I would add that it is also a picture of the achievement of object permanence, object constancy, and a good deal of capacity for symbolization, the differentiation of the internal and external world (if there is an external object, there must be a separate internal self to feel its externality), and separation of the conscious and unconscious aspects of mind. "Here fantasy begins for the individual" (p. 90).

Before this stage of object-usage, there is the "intermediate position," which is the "main theme" of Winnicott's paper. In that intermediate position "'subject destroys object.'" And "there is a price that has to be paid" (p. 90) by the subject (the infant) in the ongoing destruction of the object in unconscious fantasy. But what is the price paid by "the object," the *real* mother, an actual human being, who, unlike an internal object mother (a fantasied mother), feels the pain of being destroyed as a mother?

Winnicott does not "answer" this question, but he says something that I believe has a direct bearing on it. He does so in a sentence that I find to be pivotal to an understanding of the paper as a whole:

> This is a position [the intermediate position between object-relating and object-use] that can be arrived at by the individual in early stages of emotional growth only through the actual survival of the cathected objects that are at the time in process of becoming destroyed because real, becoming real because destroyed (being destructible and expendable).
>
> (p. 90)

This sentence is complex both in syntactical structure and in the structure of the paradox it creates. The first part of the sentence might be paraphrased as follows: object usage can be achieved early in emotional development only through the survival of the person with whom the infant or child has an emotional tie (a "cathected" object). This is a deceptively simple thought in that it seems to be a repetition of what has already been said: object-usage can be achieved only through the survival of the object. However, the words that stand out for me in this part of the sentence are: "actual survival." Winnicott is not speaking metaphorically: the object is liable to *in fact (in reality) not survive emotionally (and perhaps also physically)*.

The sentence continues with a set of ideas that I find to be the most original in the paper: the actual survival of the object is critical at this moment when the mother is "in process of *becoming destroyed because real, becoming real because destroyed*" (emphasis added). My mind reels, even now, when I read these words. I have spent many hours trying to do something with—come to my own understanding of—this pair of ideas. What does it mean to say that the object is "becoming destroyed because [it is] real"? Here, one has no choice but to "write" Winnicott's paper because he leaves critically important ideas in a highly elusive form—ideas not explained, merely suggested.

I would "write" this part of the paper by saying that the object—the actual living, breathing, emotionally responsive external object mother—is (inevitably, inescapably) "becoming destroyed" in the developmental process leading to the infant's achievement of object-usage. What I mean when I say that the *actual mother* is becoming destroyed is that her experience of herself as a good enough mother to her infant is under severe attack and is in the process of "becoming destroyed." Winnicott at times in this paper uses the phrase "becoming destroyed" and at other times uses the stronger single word "destroyed" to describe "the object" (the mother) at this moment in the development of the mother–infant relationship. I believe both wordings are accurate in that the mother and the infant at different points in this process feel as if the mother is being destroyed and at other times feel she has been destroyed.

Winnicott leaves unspoken the reality that something important about the mother's experience of herself (and the infant's experience of her) as a mother is *actually* destroyed in the course of the movement from object-relating to object-usage. What mother has not had the very painful experience of feeling that she has utterly failed as a mother, and what's more, she has ceased to be the person she was before she had the baby? The destruction of the mother's experience of herself as a mother may take innumerable forms, for instance, by her coming to feel that she is not fit to be a mother because she is unable to console her baby when he is in terrible distress, or is not sufficiently loving for the infant to nurse at the breast, or unable to help her infant sleep when he is so desperately in need of sleep, or hating her baby for keeping her from all of the pleasures and sources of pride and competence and creativity that she had had in her life before the baby was born, or any of a thousand other ways an infant or child may *actually* destroy his mother's belief in her adequacy as a mother (and, at times, her adequacy as a worthwhile person of any sort). The baby does not do this in an effort to attack his mother or destroy her; he does so simply by being the infant he is—an infant who places relentless physical and emotional demands on the mother, demands that no mother can meet. The mother's feeling of becoming destroyed is simply a part of the experience of being a mother to an infant or child, an experience that is at once mundane and unimaginably intense, painful, draining, gratifying, terrifying, and blissful.

The mother's feeling of "becoming destroyed" as a mother is not restricted to the early months of the life of the mother and infant. It occurs throughout the life of the mother and child (and later, the father and child), often more visible during "the terrible twos" and more violent during the child's adolescence.

The way I am conceiving of *the actual destruction of the mother* is akin to Loewald's (1979) idea of the killing of the oedipal parents, a killing that is not simply a symbolic killing:

> If we do not shrink from blunt language, in our role as children of our parents, by genuine emancipation [genuinely becoming independent adults] we do kill something vital in them—not all in one blow and not in all respects, but contributing to their dying.
>
> (p. 395)

As parents, we must allow ourselves to be killed (psychically and physically) by our children, "lest we diminish them" (Loewald, 1979, p. 395) by interfering with their achievement of autonomy. The stage of development that Loewald is addressing is much later than that involving the achievement of object-usage. Nonetheless, I believe that Loewald's conception of the realness of the destruction of the object ("we do kill something vital in them") is also true of the destruction of the mother in the ongoing process of developing the capacity for object-usage. The mother is not simply a facilitator of the infant's developing a sense of her externality (and his own internal world), she is a sacrifice to it. She must do nothing less than allow herself to be destroyed.

I will now turn to the second of the pair of phrases (actually they are two collapsed sentences): "*becoming real because destroyed*" (p. 90, emphasis added). Here, the object is "real because [the infant perceives the way in which the mother is feeling] destroyed." In other words, simultaneously with the mother becoming destroyed because she is a real person is the infant's perceiving the mother's experience of being destroyed as a mother. The infant senses the pain that his mother (as a real person, not as his omnipotent creation) *actually feels* as if she is becoming destroyed. This is a critical part of the period between object-relating and object-usage: the infant sees in his mother's eyes, hears in her voice, feels in the way she holds him the pain she is experiencing as she is "becoming destroyed."

Nothing is more important to an infant or child than his mother's conscious and unconscious emotional state to which he is exquisitely sensitive (Beebe and Lachmann, 2004; Fraiberg, 1980; Green, 1986; Winnicott, 1960, 1963). The infant's registering, and responding emotionally, to his mother's pain as she is "becoming destroyed" (as

82

she is coming to feel unfit to be a mother) is an essential part of the "intermediate position" between object-relating and object-usage. The mother "becom[es] real because destroyed" in that she becomes real to the infant because her feelings of "becoming destroyed" are becoming real to him.

At the same time, the mother is "in process" of *surviving because real*. She is able to survive destruction *because* she is a real person—an adult with mature (as well as primitive) emotions, ideas, and psychological capacities of her own, which she is able to bring to bear on the experience of *actually being destroyed* as a mother and of *actually surviving* as she is becoming destroyed. In other words, she, as a mature subject separate from the infant, may be able to survive feeling she is a mother in name only; she does so by mobilizing her own (real) conscious and unconscious capacities to recover her sense of herself as a good enough mother, even as she is "becoming destroyed" as a good enough mother.

If the mother and infant are to succeed in negotiating this emotional terrain, the mother must not only survive the pain of becoming destroyed, she must also communicate her survival. She makes this communication in the myriad ways in which she is genuinely alive and loving in her way of being with her baby—which the infant awaits anxiously (after he destroys her) and celebrates when he finds it.

Other people in the mother's life may be able to help her to survive becoming destroyed, for example, her husband, her mother, her grandmother, her analyst—who may be able to give her literal and/or figurative periods of rest or sleep during which "to dream" (Bion, 1962; Ogden, 2004)—to do unconscious psychological work with—the experience of being destroyed by her infant, and the experience of surviving that destruction. The mother may also be helped to survive as she is being destroyed by the felt presence of unconscious internal objects derived from actual experience with people who took care of her when she was an infant and child, and who managed to survive all the while they were being destroyed by her.

The syntax of the portion of the sentence under discussion—"in process of becoming destroyed because real, becoming real because destroyed"—is significant in that the verb *to destroy* is twice used in the passive voice (destroyed). By eliminating both the subject (the infant) and the active form of the verb (destroys), "destruction," in the sentence, simply "turns up" (p. 91). Implied is the idea that the infant does not intentionally destroy the object; rather, as Winnicott puts it much later in the paper, "destruction turns up and becomes a central feature so far as the object is objectively perceived" (p. 91). In this way, Winnicott subtly introduces an idea by means of syntactical structure, thus allowing the reader to live with it, before he puts it into more explanatory words.

The sentence being discussed concludes with the parenthetical statement that the object that is becoming real in the process of becoming destroyed is also becoming "destructible and expendable." In other words, the mother's "destruction" and survival of that destruction promotes the infant's feeling sufficiently secure to be able to experience her as expendable, superfluous, unnecessary, beside the point. He knows she will survive the experience of becoming expendable.

Just as the mother's ability to stay alive for herself and for the infant while becoming destroyed is the lynchpin of the process of the infant's developing the capacity to use objects, in the analytic setting,

> the analyst, the analytic technique, and the analytic setting all come in as surviving or not surviving the patient's destructive attacks. This destructive activity is the patient's attempt to place the analyst outside the area of omnipotent control, that is, out in the world. Without the experience of maximum destructiveness (object not protected) the subject never places the analyst outside and therefore can never do more than experience a kind of self-analysis, using the analyst as a projection of part of the self.
>
> (p. 91)

Winnicott's language is stronger here. The analyst must survive "maximum destructiveness (object not protected)." In other words, the analyst must not impede the patient's destructive attacks, nor should he become defensive, for instance, by the defensive use of interpretations that attempt to defuse the intensity of the patient's feelings. (This is the allusion, to which I earlier referred, to the idea that "It appalls me to think how much deep change I have prevented or delayed in patients ... by my personal need to interpret," p. 86.) It is important not to equate destructiveness with anger in this passage. The patient need not feel angry as he is ignoring or dismissing the analyst or making him feel superfluous. The urge to retaliate on the part of the mother/analyst is fully understandable—we all, as parents and as analysts, have felt the impulse to retaliate in the face of repeated experiences of becoming destroyed as parents and as analysts. But there are periods in the process of moving from object-relating to object-usage during which retaliation of any sort is experienced by the infant or patient as an attack on his sanity (more accurately, his psyche-soma). Under these circumstances, the mother's/analyst's actual retaliation sets in motion a pathogenic process that may be irreversible if not identified and addressed thoughtfully and cogently.

> These attacks may be very difficult for the analyst to stand, especially when they are expressed in terms of delusion, or through manipulation which makes the analyst actually do things that are technically bad. (I refer to such a thing as being unreliable at moments when reliability is all that matters, as well as to survival in terms of keeping alive and of absence of the quality of retaliation.)
>
> (p. 92)

In this passage, Winnicott addresses for the first time the actual pain the analyst (and by extension, the mother) feels in response to being destroyed as an analyst by the patient, but he stops short of identifying the patient's perception of, and response to, the analyst's pain as a principal medium through which the analyst/mother becomes real for the patient/infant. As I have discussed, I believe the patient's/infant's perception of, and response to, the pain of the analyst/mother are critical to the movement from object-relating to object-usage.

To summarize, the idea that the mother is "becoming destroyed because real" suggests to me that the mother can only become destroyed *because she is real*—a real person who is able to experience the pain of being destroyed as an adequate mother. And she is "becoming real because destroyed" in that the infant is able to sense the reality of the pain she experiences (as a separate person) in becoming destroyed (as a mother). Moreover, she *survives because real* in that only a real person living in the world external to the infant's subjectivity is able to be destroyed and at the same time survive as a

85

living presence who continues to love her infant, and continues to be emotionally present for him, and able to dream (to do the necessary unconscious psychological work with) the experience of being destroyed and of surviving being destroyed.

Not quite finished: a theoretical point

Winnicott opens the final portion of the paper with a personal statement reminiscent of the writing in the opening section. He says,

> I have now nearly made my whole statement. Not quite however, because it is not possible for me to take for granted an acceptance [on the part of the reader] of the fact that the first impulse in the subject's relation to the object (objectively perceived, not subjective) is destructive [but that destructiveness is *not* an aggressive response to reality].
>
> (p. 90)

And later, he elaborates:

> The assumption is always there, in orthodox theory, that aggression is reactive to the encounter with the reality principle, whereas here [between object-relating and object usage] it is the destructive drive that creates the quality of externality. This is essential in the structure of my argument.
>
> (p. 93)

Winnicott is very concerned that his use of the term "destruction" will lead the reader to believe that he views the infant as reacting to reality with aggression. For Winnicott, it is the other way round: destruction is not a response to reality, it "creates" reality ("the quality of externality"):

> The central postulate in this [his own] thesis is that, whereas the subject does not destroy the subjective object (projection material), destruction turns up and becomes a central feature so far as the object is objectively perceived, has autonomy, and belongs to "shared" reality.
>
> (p. 91)

As I mentioned earlier, I have come to realize something about Winnicott's paper that I have not until now quite named for myself: he is inventing a meaning for the word *destruction* that differs both from its meaning in general usage and from the way any other psychoanalyst has used it. But the meaning of the term is elusive because Winnicott never defines it; instead, he conveys its meaning only by the way he uses the term in the sentences he writes. Moreover, the term acquires different inflections of meaning as the paper unfolds.

What Winnicott does with the word *destruction*—reinventing it, defining it only through the way he uses it, and allowing it to accrue new meanings as he proceeds—contributes to making this paper extremely difficult to understand and impossible to paraphrase. Consequently, it is necessary for me to create my own understandings of the term *destruction*. The meanings I make will be different from those you, the reader, will make, and different from the ones I will make when reading Winnicott's paper tomorrow.

To return to the text, in the second of the passages just cited, Winnicott uses the phrase "destruction turns up" (to which I referred earlier), which I view as an elegant way of expressing the idea that the infant destroys the mother without anger and without the intention of destroying her. Destruction "turns up" because a healthy infant or child asks (demands!) a great deal from his or her mother, more than any mother can provide.

The reader must hold this use of the term *destruction* in mind when later Winnicott speaks of "the patient's destructive attacks" (p. 91) that the analyst must survive. The two phrases—"destruction turns up" and "the patient's destructive attacks"—become, in Winnicott's hands, coexisting facets of "destruction," both of which describe aspects of the process in which the infant or patient "creates externality." Destruction may take the form of attack when the patient (or infant) feels trapped in a solipsistic, confining world and feels "the drive" (p. 93) to battle his way into external reality. Even when engaging in "destructive attacks" (p. 91) "on the analyst, the analytic technique, and the analytic setting" (p. 91), Winnicott insists, "*There is no anger* in the destruction of the object" (p. 93, original emphasis). Destruction simply turns up in the mother–infant relationship as the infant is driven (in health) toward object-usage.

> It will be seen that, although destruction is the word I am using, this actual destruction belongs to the object's failure to survive.

> Without this failure, destruction remains potential. The word "destruction" is needed, not because of the baby's impulse to destroy, but because of the object's liability not to survive, which also means to suffer change in quality, in attitude.
>
> (p. 93)

In the first two of these sentences, Winnicott uses the term "failure to survive"; in the third, he uses the term "liability not to survive." I find the phrase, "liability not to survive," a description more accurate than "failure to survive" (because of the judgmental connotations of the word *failure*) when referring to a breakdown in the relationship between mother and infant. I believe that it is crucial that we, as analysts, not become judgmental about the mother's (or our own) liability not to survive destruction.

It is not easy being a mother or being an analyst, particularly when one is becoming destroyed. Winnicott, in his BBC radio broadcasts and in the books he wrote for the general public (Winnicott, 1969b), tried to help mothers and fathers become more accepting of themselves as parents (including their feelings of anger and defeat at the hands of their infant). In his paper, "Hate in the countertransference" (1947), Winnicott attempts to do something similar for analysts. Perhaps most analysts have the humility to admit that they are not able to be of help to every patient they accept for analysis. What is more difficult to admit is that there are times when we, as analysts, are unable to survive destruction in an analysis we are conducting, and yet, to the detriment of the patient and ourselves, we continue to work with the patient (sometimes without seeking consultation or further personal analysis). I will discuss this aspect of analytic work in greater detail in the clinical portion of this paper.

Before turning to clinical work, I would like to make explicit a theoretical point that Winnicott does not address. The achievement of object-usage, as I understand it, does not only involve a state of mind that "creates the quality of externality" (p. 93), it also involves a state of mind that creates the unconscious mind itself (in the sense that the conscious mind becomes differentiated from the unconscious mind). When the infant is in the stage of object-relating, there is not yet a conscious and an unconscious mind: the infant cannot differentiate his thoughts and feelings from his perceptions of the world. With the achievement of object-use, unconscious fantasy comes into being ("Here fantasy begins for the individual," p. 90).

Having said that the discovery of externality allows for the differentiation of the conscious and unconscious aspects of mind, I must add that I disagree with Winnicott's notion that the destruction of the mother continues "all the time ... in (unconscious) *fantasy*" (p. 90, original emphasis), an idea that he later states in slightly different words: "the object is *in fantasy* always being destroyed" (p. 93, original emphasis). By contrast, in my conception of the "destruction of the mother" during the "intermediate position" between object-relating and object-usage, the experience of the mother's destruction and her survival are not unconscious fantasies, they are realities that the mother experiences, and that the infant perceives and responds to. The infant's perception of the mother's destruction (his perception of her feeling that she is failing as a mother) and the infant's perception of her survival as his mother are both real, and are both critical to the process by which the infant "creates externality." Because these experiences of destruction and survival are real, they continue not in "unconscious *fantasy*," but in *unconscious memory elaborated in fantasy*. What I mean by *unconscious memory elaborated in fantasy* is the registration in unconscious memory of an *actual* experience, which is then elaborated in unconscious fantasy and persists as a "backcloth" (p. 94) of "ongoing destruction [of the object] in unconscious fantasy" (p. 90). I also include in the psychic registrations of actual past events those past events that are *not experienced* at the time they occur because they are more than the individual can manage psychically. Those not yet experienced psychic registrations are "waiting" for circumstances (a holding, containing environment such as that created in the analytic setting) in which portions of one's "unlived life" (Ogden, 2014) might be lived/experienced (Winnicott, 1974; Faimberg, 1998 [2013]).

Two clinical discussions

Playing doctor

Mr. B, a man in his late forties, came to analysis saying that he "needed help" with problems in his life that now seemed "beyond repair." He could not be specific about what the problems were, but the feeling he mentioned most often was "despair." As if complying with what he thought I expected of him, he told me about his parents and siblings, but did so in a way that gave me almost no sense of who these people really were. The one exception was his description of his younger sister who was addicted to alcohol and drugs, had a small child, and was at times homeless. She refused help of any kind.

As Mr. B told me about his sister, an image came to mind of a girl climbing over the railing of the Golden Gate Bridge in the process of killing herself. My mind drifted to the thought that the news media do not report the suicides committed by jumping from the bridge because, I imagined, to report these suicides would be to collude with the person's wish for a moment of recognition, evidence in print that this person had once existed, and due to terrible pain, had ended his or her life. I suspected that there was a form of recognition that Mr. B needed with such intensity that he would give up his life (or mine) to attain it. I felt that to begin analysis with him was to take on a potentially suicidal (or homicidal) patient.

I said to Mr. B, "I think that you want me to know that something went terribly wrong in your family and that the pain resulting from it has been unbearable."

Mr. B said in a flat tone of voice, "I suppose that's true for my sister."

I later in the session said to the patient, "I suspect that coming to see me about beginning analysis is one of the most difficult things you've done in your life."

He paused and said, "Oh," in a way that made me feel, for the first time in the session, that he and I had made an emotional connection, albeit a very fragile one. It was only then that I decided to work with Mr. B in analysis.

In the early years of analysis, Mr. B told me that his mother dressed bizarrely and would say nonsensical things while standing alone in the middle of a room. He numbed himself to her and never invited anyone to his house so he "wouldn't have to see her through their eyes." He spent most of his time by himself either in his room or in the fields behind his house. His sister, three years younger, had "joined forces" with their mother, telling their mother every detail of her day, which their mother "drank up."

During these initial years, I felt I was learning "about" the patient's life, but I did not really know him, and he did not really know me. I was patient with Mr. B, always cognizant of his fear of revealing his mother's psychosis, and his own. The patient, one day, began the session by saying that there was something he had been wanting to tell me, but had been too ashamed to do so. He said that he and his sister had "played doctor" when he was eight years old and she was five. Mr. B sobbed as he told me about looking at, but not touching, his sister's genitals. He was as frightened as he was curious. He said that he knew that he had caused her "lasting damage."

After Mr. B told me his "shameful secret," I had the feeling that he was going to prematurely end the analysis, now that some of the weight of that secret was off his shoulders. Though he was experiencing some relief from his feelings of despair, I felt that in many ways he was absent from his own analysis. The two of us rarely talked in a way that felt alive to me. When I spoke, my voice often sounded to me strangely thin and insubstantial. Most of the time during our sessions, I felt lost and directionless. Mr. B had been a prolific dreamer in the early part of the analysis, and there had been, at times, a feeling of discovery that we shared as we talked about them, but he had not told me a dream in a very long time.

Although I did not connect this with my work with Mr. B, I became alarmed when I began to feel, while consulting to analysts on their work with psychotic patients, that I used to do that kind of work but no longer did. I was sailing along on reputation, rather than on genuine expertise. In short, I was a fraud. This was a profoundly disturbing feeling that carried over into other sectors of my life.

During this period Mr. B arrived late for several sessions in a row, which was unprecedented for him. On each of these days, upon opening the door to the waiting room, I could feel the patient's gaze wash over my face in a scrutinizing way. He had almost always kept his eyes to the floor when I met him. I wondered if he sensed that something was upsetting me and that he was late to his sessions in an effort to help me by giving me "a rest" from dealing with him.

At the beginning of one of these sessions, my mind returned to the patient's account of "playing doctor" with his sister. I began to think of it differently. It now seemed to me that the "lasting damage" to which the patient referred may have more to do with the damage he had suffered early on at the hands of his psychotic mother than it had to do with the damage he had done to his sister. I suspected that the patient had been trying to tell me something very personal and important to him, and I had not been able to fully hear it until now: his terrible secret about playing doctor was a disguised version, almost a dream image, of his attempt to be a doctor to his mother in an effort to cure her of her psychosis.

In this more deeply unconscious story/dream image of "playing doctor" with his mother, he is curious and frightened as he looks into her psychotic internal world, but does not dare to enter, for if he does enter, he, like his sister, would never escape, and would become as lost as his sister was. I thought that despite "knowing this," Mr. B felt profound sadness and guilt regarding his failure to be a doctor to his mother (and his very disturbed sister), and it was these failures that were his terrible secret.

I recognized at this point that my own feelings of being a failure (what I would now call "my feelings of being destroyed") as a doctor resonated with those of the patient. I was not (in feeling) a real doctor, I was a fraud—I was only "playing doctor," as he had done with his sister and (in unconscious fantasy) with his mother. I felt considerable relief as I came to view my painful feelings of failure and fraudulence as a medium in which Mr. B was trying to communicate something crucially important to him.

While with Mr. B during this period, a memory came to me. A very close elderly friend had been in hospice care for a few months during which time she would awaken for only very short periods of time before falling back into a sleep that did not seem like ordinary sleep. During one of my visits, I asked her if she dreamt while she slept. After a long pause, she responded, "I don't dream, thank God."

Without planning to do so, I said to Mr. B, "I miss your dreams."

He replied, through choked tears, "I do too."

I will try not to destroy the clinical experience I have just described by offering explanations. The experience about which I wrote (more accurately, the experience I wrote) came to mind almost immediately in connection with Winnicott's ideas, my ideas, our ideas. What I wrote is not an illustration, much less evidence of or proof of anything, but there are connections in my mind, and perhaps now in yours. Instead of an explanation, I will offer some impressions.

Psychosis appeared almost immediately in the first meeting in the form of the patient's sister. And with it, fear: his fear of his mother's deadly psychosis, my fear of his deadly psychosis, his fear of my deadly psychosis. And on its heels came failure: his failure to cure his mother, my failure to cure him, our failure to wake up. There was also a good deal of aloneness: his and mine; and there developed, along the way, loneliness: his, mine, ours. Tenderness appeared: his noticing my distress, my noticing his noticing, and his noticing my noticing his noticing. And there were words: "I miss your dreams," I miss you, I love you, "I do too."

The analyst who is unable to survive being destroyed

I have had quite a number of analysts consult with me over the years about analyses in which they are having great difficulty surviving destruction. I must speak in general terms because I am unable to disguise these cases sufficiently to ensure the confidentiality of the patient and analyst. The analyst is almost always in a state of great distress about an analysis, which he says (and I usually come to concur) is not representative of his work as an analyst. I feel compassion for both patient and analyst who find themselves in this situation and respect the analyst for bringing into consultation a situation that he almost always experiences as shameful.

Winnicott does not mince words regarding the difficulty of the analyst's task of helping the patient create "externality itself" (p. 91):

> Without the experience of *maximum destructiveness (object not protected)* the subject never places the analyst outside and therefore can never experience more than a kind of self-analysis, using the analyst as a projection of a part of the self.
>
> (p. 91, emphasis added)

I enter into consultation to an analyst with humility. After all, the analyst knows the analysand far better than I do. If, after a series of consultation meetings, I feel that I may be able to be of some value to the analyst and his patient, we begin weekly consultation in which we focus on the analyst's *experience* (as opposed to his understanding) of what is happening between the patient and himself.

In these consultations concerning the analyst's experience of being unable to survive in the analytic relationship, I find that the analyst regularly feels under attack by the patient.

> These attacks may be very difficult for the analyst to stand, especially when they are expressed in terms of delusion, or

93

through manipulation which make the analyst actually do things that are technically bad.

(Winnicott, 1971, p. 92)

Highly significant is the footnote that Winnicott appends to the clause, "These attacks may be very difficult for the analyst to stand":

When the analyst knows that the patient carries a revolver, then, it seems to me, this work cannot be done.

(1971, p. 92, fn. 1)

With Winnicott's words in mind, I am attentive to the possible psychic reality on the part of the analyst that the patient carries a figurative revolver, i.e., that the patient has the capacity to kill him not only psychically, but physically. For the purpose of further helping the analyst gain greater access to his own unconscious psychic reality, I strongly recommend that he resume his personal analysis while working out his difficulty in working with his patient.

In consulting to an analyst who is feeling destroyed, I pay close attention not only to the emotional states of the analyst and his patient, but also to their physical state. This, to my mind, is a critical measure of the degree of destruction occurring in the analysis. It has been my experience that the analyst's inability to survive destruction very often involves the analyst's development of physical illness, such as severe headaches, ectopic dermatitis, and chronic insomnia. The patient, too, frequently develops forms of physical illness and self-destructive behaviors.

If, upon careful consideration, over an extended period of time, I find that the emotional and physical damage to the patient and to the analyst are severe and chronic, and continue unabated despite the analyst's in-depth work in consultation (and in some cases, personal analysis), I recommend that the analyst end his work with this patient. Such a recommendation is an extreme measure and is a rare event in my experience as a consultant.

Considerable work is involved in the analyst's formulating for himself the way he will bring the analysis to a close. I have found in the course of taking part in these consultations that it is of the utmost importance that the analyst convey to the patient (and genuinely understand, himself) that his decision to end the analysis does not mean that the patient is "unanalyzable" (unable to make use of psychoanalytic treatment); it means that *he*, the analyst, is unable to do productive analytic work with *this* patient. It is often possible for the patient to accept the analyst's help in finding another analyst with whom he or she may be able to do productive analytic work.

The idea of the patient's finding another analyst is often narcissistically wounding to patient and analyst. They both feel that they are failures—the patient imagines himself to be "an untouchable" in the eyes of prospective analysts; and the analyst imagines that the patient and the new analyst will view him as incompetent, or worse, and that word about his inadequacy as an analyst will spread to the entire analytic community. While this process of ending the analysis is extremely painful for the analytic pair, I have found that both patient and analyst (unconsciously, and also usually consciously) experience a sense of relief in ending an analysis that has not been good for either of them for a long time.

I am saddened by the experience of consulting to an analyst who has come to the conclusion that he must end an analysis in which he has been unable to survive and has retaliated in response to what he experienced as the patient's effort to destroy him. But I find it equally disturbing to work with an analyst who is unable to acknowledge his inability to survive destruction as well as his overt and covert acts of retaliation.

I have come to believe that one of an analyst's most important responsibilities to his patient is that of being able to recognize when (to face the fact that) an analysis is unremittingly destructive to his patient, and to end the analysis if he is unable to repair the situation.

Concluding comments

In my reading of Winnicott's "The use of an object," I suggest that the process in which the object is "becoming destroyed because real, becoming real because destroyed," the object (initially, the mother) is becoming destroyed because she is able to feel she is becoming destroyed emotionally (as a real person capable of the feeling of becoming destroyed as a mother). At the same time, the object (the mother) is "becoming real" for the infant in the process of perceiving *the reality of his mother's feeling destroyed* as well as perceiving *the reality of her psychic survival of that destruction*. She is able to survive "because [she is] real"—because she is able to do unconscious psychological work with her feelings of being destroyed and surviving destruction.

I also suggest that the process of attaining object-usage involves not only the creation of "the quality of externality" (p. 93), but also the creation of the unconscious mind itself (the differentiation of the conscious and unconscious aspects of mind), and the creation of the self.

I differ from Winnicott when he says that the mother continues being destroyed "all the time … in (unconscious) *fantasy*" (p. 90, original emphasis). I would say that the destruction of the mother and her survival persist not as unconscious *fantasy*, but as unconscious *memory* (*elaborated in unconscious fantasy*) of the mother's actually becoming destroyed and actually surviving destruction.

References

Beebe, B. & Lachmann, F. (2004). *The Origins of Attachment: Infant Research and Adult Treatment: Coconstructing Interactions.* London: Routledge.

Bion, W. R. (1962). *Learning from Experience.* London: Tavistock.

Faimberg, H. [1998] (2013). Nachtraglichkeit and Winnicott's "Fear of breakdown." In *Donald Winnicott Today*, edited by J. Abram, pp. 205–212. London: Routledge.

Fraiberg, S. (1980). *Clinical Studies in Infant Mental Health: The First Year of Life.* New York: Basic Books.

Green, A. (1986). The dead mother. In *On Private Madness*. Madison, CT: International Universities Press, pp. 142–174.

Loewald, H. (1979). The waning of the Oedipus complex. In *Papers on Psychoanalysis*. New Haven, CT: Yale University Press, 1980, pp. 384–484.

Ogden, T. H. (1983). The mother, the infant, and the matrix: Interpretations of aspects of the work of Donald Winnicott. *Contemporary Psychoanalysis*, 21:346–371.

Ogden, T. H. (1986). *The Matrix of the Mind: Object Relations and the Psychoanalytic Dialogue*. Northvale, NJ: Aronson.

Ogden, T. H. (2004). This art of psychoanalysis: Dreaming undreamt dreams and interrupted cries. *The International Journal of Psychoanalysis*, 85:857–878.

Ogden, T. H. (2014). Fear of breakdown and the unlived life. *The International Journal of Psychoanalysis*, 95:205–224.

Rodman, F. R. (2003). *Winnicott: Life and Work*. Cambridge, MA: Perseus Publishing.

Samuels, L. (2001). The paradox of destruction and survival in D. W. Winnicott's "The Use of an Object." *Fort Da*, 7:38–53.

Winnicott, D. W. (1947). Hate in the countertransference. In *Through Paediatrics to Psycho-Analysis*, New York: International Universities Press, 1975, pp. 194–204.

Winnicott, D. W. (1960). The theory of the parent–infant relationship. In *The Maturational Processes and the Facilitating Environment*. New York: International Universities Press, 1965, pp. 33–55.

Winnicott, D. W. (1963). From dependence towards independence in the development of the individual. In *The Maturational Processes and the Facilitating Environment*. New York: International Universities Press, 1965, pp. 83–92.

Winnicott, D. W. (1969a). The use of an object and relating through identifications. *The International Journal of Psychoanalysis*, 50:711–716.

Winnicott, D. W. (1969b). *The Child, the Parent, and the Outside World*. New York: Penguin.

Winnicott, D. W. (1971). The use of an object and relating through identifications. In *Playing and Reality*. New York: Basic Books, 1971, pp. 86–94.

Winnicott, D. W. [1971] 1974. Fear of breakdown. In *Psychoanalytic Explorations*, edited by C. Winnicott, R. Shepherd, and M. Davis. Cambridge, MA: Harvard University Press, 1989, pp. 87–95.

5

DREAMING THE ANALYTIC SESSION

A clinical essay

Introduction

The idea of dreaming the analytic session is, for me, one of the most important and one of the most difficult of psychoanalytic concepts. It is a way of conceptualizing a fundamental aspect of the way I practice psychoanalysis, which I must rediscover again and again. The concept is impossible to pin down, which is a reflection of how full of life it can be, and how mysterious and elusive it can be.

This chapter is predominantly clinical in nature, but my experience *during* analytic sessions is not separable from the way I *think about* analytic sessions. So before I describe experiences of dreaming analytic sessions with three of my patients, I will offer a very brief discussion of elements of the theoretical framework that I bring to my clinical work. I see analytic theory not as a set of laws, but as a set of metaphors that I use to describe, not explain, for myself (during and after a session) the events of the session. As is the case with all metaphors, analytic theories/metaphors reach a breaking point and must be replaced by fresh metaphors.

Theory

I initially encountered the concept of dreaming the analytic session in Bion's work. He mentions the idea of dreaming the session in entries in *Cogitations* (1992): "These events [of the session] are having something done to them mentally, and that which is being done is what I call being dreamed" ([undated], 1992, p. 39). "The analyst must be able to dream the session" ([undated], 1992, p. 120). And:

DOI: 10.4324/9781003228462-5

[There is] a felt need to convert the conscious rational experience into dream, rather than a felt need to convert the dream
into conscious rational experience. The "felt need" is *very*
important; if it is not given due significance and weight, the
true dis-ease of the patient is being neglected; it is obscured by
the analyst's insistence on interpretation of the dream.

([August 1960], 1992, p. 184,
original emphasis)

Putting this last passage into my own words, with my own elabo-
rations: when the analyst dreams the events of the session with the
patient, he transforms consciously perceived experience into unconscious experience. A revolutionary thought is being introduced here:
dreaming is not a process of making the unconscious conscious, as
Freud (1900) would have it; it is, for Bion, a process of making
the conscious unconscious, a process of transforming "conscious,
rational" experiences with external objects into internal object
relationships, thereby making experiences organized by means of
conscious, secondary process thinking available for unconscious
psychological work.

Thus, the analyst, in his role as analyst, experiences a "felt need"
to dream the events of the session. Dreaming the session is stifled by
the analyst's "interpretation of the dream," that is, by the analyst's
premature need to make the unconscious conscious by means of
verbal symbolization. In still other words: it all starts with conscious,
lived experience that is rendered unconscious so that something can
be done with it mentally by means of dreaming (unconscious thinking). Only at that point is the unconscious understanding of lived
experience *sometimes* made conscious by means of interpretation.

In the tradition of Bion (1962a, 1987, 1992), I think of dreaming
as synonymous with unconscious thinking. Unconscious thinking
(*dream thinking* [Ogden, 2010]) is our richest form of thinking. It
continues uninterrupted both while we are awake and while we
are asleep, just as the stars continue to emit light even when that
light is rendered invisible by the glare of the sun. Dream thinking
is a form of thinking in which experience is viewed from multiple
vertices simultaneously: for example, from the vertex of primary *and*
secondary process thinking; from the perspective of mature sym-
bol formation *and* symbolic equation; from the viewpoint of paranoid schizoid *and* depressive *and* autistic-contiguous (Ogden, 1989)

99

modes of generating experience; from the vantage point of adult constructions of life events *and* childhood constructions of life events; from the perspective of a diachronic (sequential) *and* a synchronic (ahistorical) sense of time; from the vertex of linear cause-and-effect thinking *and* of nonlinear thinking—to name only a few. (For a fuller discussion of Bion's conception of dreaming, see Ogden [2003, 2004a].)

I view dreaming (unconscious thinking) as *inherently therapeutic*; it constitutes the core of what Bion (1962a) calls the "psychoanalytic function of the personality" (p. 89). He writes, "without dreams you have not the means to think out your emotional problems" (1967, p. 25). Freud concurs: "At bottom, dreams are nothing other than a particular *form* of thinking, made possible by the conditions of the state of sleep. … Dreams concern themselves with attempts at solving the problems by which our mental life is faced" (1900, pp. 506–507, original emphasis).

One need not remember one's dreams for them to serve the psychoanalytic function of self-understanding, which is an underpinning of psychological growth. Grotstein (2000) describes the psychoanalytic function of dreaming as a mutually enriching conversation between the unconscious dreamer who dreams the dream and the unconscious dreamer who understands the dream. Sandler (1976) describes that psychoanalytic function as an interplay of the unconscious *dream-work* and the unconscious *understanding-work*.

Dreaming, as is the case with self-understanding achieved in the course of an analytic session, does not succeed in "solving the [emotional] problems" (Freud, 1900, pp. 506–507) all at once. Rather, dreaming *contributes* to solving emotional problems bit by bit, without ever reaching an endpoint ("the solution"). If one is not changed, even in the most modest of ways, by the experience of dreaming a dream, I would view this "dream" as a dream that is not a dream; rather it is an unconscious event cast in the form of visual images that achieves no unconscious psychological work and does not lead to psychic growth. Dreams that are not dreams include "dreams" to which no associations can be made by patient or analyst, hallucinations in sleep, and post-traumatic nightmares that are repeated night after night without change in the dreamer.

Psychic health, to my mind, is a reflection of the degree to which a person is able to genuinely engage in dreaming his lived experience. Being able to dream one's experience "completely" is not only impossible; it is also undesirable in that the person would become inhuman: he or she would have no psychic problems to work on.

From this perspective, psychoanalysis long pre-dates Freud. It began as a human need for self-understanding (a form of the human need for truth [Bion, 1992, p. 99]) in the service of psychological growth unconsciously mediated by the experience of dreaming. Dreaming in this way creates the differentiation of the conscious and unconscious aspects of mind, which is inseparable from the achievement of human consciousness (Bion, 1962a). Psychoanalysis was, for millennia, a thought without a thinker, until Freud was able to think it (more accurately, until Freud was able to write it [Civitarese, 2013]).

As I mentioned earlier, we are all the time engaged in dreaming, both when we are awake and when we are asleep (Bion, 1962a). On waking, we remember only a tiny fraction of the dreams we have dreamt, but the dreams we do not remember contribute to psychological growth as much as those we recall. Dreaming—whether or not we are able to remember the dream on waking—is an attempt at self-understanding, which if successful leads to psychic growth. The degree to which the dreamer is successful in achieving self–understanding and psychological growth in the process of dreaming depends on two factors: first, the degree of development of the individual's capacity to unconsciously contain/think (Bion, 1962a, 1970; Ogden, 2004b) his lived experience; and second, the help the individual may receive (for example, from the mother or analyst) in containing (in a state of reverie) his unthinkable/undreamable thoughts, and transforming them into a thought/feeling that he may be able to think/feel on his own (Bion, 1962b).

When an individual is unable to dream a lived experience, this is not a reflection of a cessation of unconscious thinking; rather, it reflects the fact that aspects of the patient's unconscious have been cut off from unconscious thinking by such means as dissociation and other radical forms of splitting–off aspects of the self (as is the case in my third clinical illustration in this chapter). These split-off, "unthinkable" aspects of the unconscious are the stuff of night-terrors—dreams that are not dreams (which I will discuss shortly).

The beginning of the reintegration of split-off (unthought/undreamt) aspects of self is always disturbing to the patient's psychic equilibrium—often to the extent that the psyche is threatened with fragmentation (as in the second clinical illustration that I will present). Depending on the strength of the patient's personality structure and the degree and type of help he is receiving, the outcome of the integration process differs greatly and in a way that is difficult to anticipate.

Dreaming while awake (waking-dreaming) in the consulting room occurs largely in the form of the analyst's and the patient's reveries. Waking-dreaming allows the analyst to "catch the drift" (Freud, 1923, p. 239) of what is occurring unconsciously at any given moment in the analytic session. Reverie, as I understand it, comes unbidden in mundane forms, such as thoughts about an argument with one's spouse, the lyrics of a song, thoughts and feelings about a recent fall taken by one's two-year-old child, childhood memories, grocery lists, and so on (Ogden, 1994). The analyst is tempted to disregard such thoughts because they usually feel like the analyst's own "stuff," but if he ignores these thoughts and feelings, he is squandering the opportunity to dream the session *with the patient.*

I view reverie as an unconscious construction of patient and analyst who together create an unconscious third subject (the *analytic third*) who is the dreamer of reveries, which are experienced by patient and analyst through the lens of their own separate (conscious and unconscious) subjectivities (Ogden, 1994). The analyst speaks to the patient almost always *from* the feeling tone and imagery of his reverie experience, not *about* it (Ogden, 1997).

In my own efforts to describe the psychoanalytic enterprise (Ogden, 2004a, 2005), I have found it useful to think of patient and analyst as engaged in a process in which the analyst contributes to the patient's development of the capacity to dream (to do unconscious psychological work with) the disturbing emotional experiences that the patient is unable to handle on his own. Often the patient is able to partially dream his experience (both while asleep and awake), but reaches a point at which the experience he is dreaming becomes so disturbing that his dreaming is interrupted, and he "wakes up" in a state of fright from his "nightmare." Symptom formation occurs at the point at which the individual is no longer able to dream his experience. Such experiences of "waking up" from the dreaming in which patient and analyst are engaged in a session reflect the fact that the dream experience has become too disturbing for one or both members of the analytic pair to bear (see the first clinical example in this chapter for an illustration of this type of dream–disruption).

Alternatively, the patient may not be able to dream his experience at all, in which case he is in a state comparable to that of a night-terror in which he cannot be awoken from his dreamless sleep, a sleep in which he is able to do no psychological work with the disturbing (often terrifying) emotional experience. The individual is able to genuinely wake up from a night-terror only when he becomes able (often with the help of the analyst) to dream his terrifying experience (his undreamt dream) in the analytic session.

Psychic states equivalent to night-terrors (undreamt dreams) and to nightmares (interrupted dreams) are the backcloth of every analysis. The analyst makes use of his own capacities for dreaming the emotional experience that is occurring in the session to facilitate the patient's efforts to dream his undreamable or incompletely dreamable dreams. This experience of analyst and patient dreaming together the patient's formerly undreamt or partially dreamt dreams constitutes one way I have of conceiving of the analytic process (Ogden, 2004a). Undreamt dreams comprise as-yet "unlived life" (Ogden, 2014)—events that took place in the patient's life at a time when he was unable to be emotionally present at the event because it would have been too disturbing to do so (Winnicott, 1971).

Practice

In the three clinical discussions that follow, no overarching theoretical principle or technique will emerge concerning a "technique" for dreaming the analytic session. I do not believe that this represents a failure to perceive an underlying pattern. Quite the contrary: the experiences of dreaming the session that I will describe are unique to each of the analytic pairs and comprise what is most alive, most true, most surprising, most growth-promoting, most difficult, most painful in these sessions.

The phone call

In the initial years of analysis, Ms. T spoke primarily about her great disappointment in herself as a mother, as a wife, and as a corporate executive. She had two children whom she said she loved but felt that there was something missing in her relationship with them. She felt ashamed of the fact that even when she was attending a sports event or theater production in which one of her children was participating, her mind was elsewhere, usually ruminating about problems at work.

Ms. T did not seem to expect or want anything from me other than my being there to listen. Vacation breaks did not appear to bother her. She would say that she hoped that it would not hurt my feelings if she told me that she was glad to save the money she spent on analysis while I was away.

As the analysis proceeded, Ms. T became increasingly despairing. At times, she wished she were dead so she could put a stop to the constant reminders of her failings. Ms. T had very few dreams, and the ones she did have seemed no different from thoughts she had while awake. For instance, she dreamt about being fired and feeling humiliated as her colleagues watched her pack up the items on her desk—a scene she often imagined and believed was about to happen in waking life. These dreams elicited in me thoughts that felt stale— ideas that felt like an imitation of analysis.

Most of our sessions began with a five- or ten-minute period of silence during which Ms. T shifted uncomfortably on the couch. These silences were painfully empty. Sometimes during these silences, I would think of events in the patient's childhood, as if searching for something that held emotional meaning: her alcoholic parents arguing and screaming at one another when drunk; her father's slamming doors that made such a loud sound that the patient thought that "the house was exploding"; her mother's perennially buying mail-order clothes and shoes she never wore.

It had been painful for Ms. T to tell me anything about her childhood. This handful of memories was almost all of what she had told me about her life growing up. These bits and pieces of Ms. T's past felt like a small collection of stones that a child might give to a parent for safekeeping. I felt honored to have been given them but did not know what to do with them (how to make analytic use of them).

One afternoon in the third year of the analysis, Ms. T was late for her session, which was highly unusual for her. As I do when patients are late for a session, I view the session as having begun at the scheduled time, even though the patient has (unconsciously) "chosen" not to be in the consulting room with me for that part of the session. As I wait for the patient, I often take "process notes" in which I write down what I feel is occurring in the session. In the process notes that I took while waiting for Ms. T, I wrote, "The room seems misshapen, as if it's being stretched from within. Will it burst? Delayed by a traffic jam? Accident? Not worried. A little worried. Very worried." There was pressure building in me and in the analytic relationship of an intensity I was not fully aware of at the time (as reflected in the image of the consulting room being stretched to its breaking point and the thought of a traffic accident).

I heard Ms. T walking quickly, heavy-footedly down the passageway leading to my waiting room about fifteen minutes after the session began. When I opened the door to the waiting room, Ms. T was standing not far from the door. Her hair was in a tangle and her coat partially buttoned—and partially incorrectly buttoned in a way that made her look a bit like a little girl. On entering the consulting room, she smoothed her dress with quick strokes of her hands, as if brushing off debris. On lying down on the couch, she said, "I'm sorry for being late. There was a report I had to finish."

I felt that we both knew that, while she was not lying, she was not telling a fuller truth about what had occurred during the initial part of the analytic session (before she arrived at my office).

A short time later, the patient's cell phone began buzzing in her handbag. To my great surprise, Ms. T, without explanation, sat up, picked up her handbag from the floor, and dipped her hand into the darkness of the interior of the bag. On finding her phone, she lifted it out of the bag and let the bag fall to the floor with a thud.

Ms. T then swiped her forefinger across the phone's face with a gesture that seemed to be at once sensuous and a slap across the face. She pulled herself to a sitting position on the couch, put the phone to her ear, and said, "Hello" in a high-pitched tone, as if forcing air through her constricted windpipe. Ms. T responded to the caller with a dozen or so "Uh-huhs" and occasional short sentences (mostly questions), such as: "Why?" "Say that again." "No." "I don't understand." "How come?"

As the phone conversation went on, I heard a pleading tone in the patient's voice that caused me to feel profoundly sad. I had previously felt sorry for her, but this feeling of sadness was different. An image came to mind of a child of five or six standing at the curb of an elementary school, the one I had attended, standing by herself or himself—the gender of the child was not well defined. All the other children had been picked up by their mothers. The child was standing alone, cold and frightened. Teachers and other adults had disappeared. There was a pay phone, but the child did not know how to use it.

An older boy or a man was now present. The child was both relieved and frightened to see this person. The child asked him for directions so she (he) could walk home. I felt an ache in my stomach that was the ache I had felt as a child when I was terrified.

Still in the grip of this reverie, I was startled when Ms. T said to me, "Sorry about the call. Where was I?"

Not knowing what I was going to say until I heard the words leave my mouth, I said, "As you were talking, I had a daydream. There was a little girl waiting for someone to pick her up after school let out. It was a windy, cold day. All the other children were gone. She looked for her teacher, but she, too, was gone. The girl tried to use the pay phone but couldn't get it to work. The child was terrified."

I regretted saying what I had said as soon as I finished saying it. I very rarely tell patients the content of my reverie experience. I asked myself why I had done so in this instance.

Before I could get my balance, Ms. T said, "You're scaring me."

I said, "I know I am." In the brief silence that followed, it struck me that the childhood scene of feeling lost, frightened, and impossibly cut off was very much like a feeling that I had been experiencing in response to the recent death of a very close friend.

Ms. T said, "It wasn't the story about the girl that scared me—it was your telling me the story that scared me. It was you but not you who was talking, because you've never told me a story before. I've never heard you talk that way." I was reminded of Ms. T's parents arguing and slamming doors when they were drunk—yelling things the patient had never heard before, being people the patient did not know.

We were silent for about a minute. During the silence, I felt that in telling the patient my reverie, I had blurred the boundary between her and me. I felt like apologizing to her, but thought that while doing so might relieve me of some of my feelings of guilt, I would be cutting short the patient's telling me her fears about me and her anger at me.

"Are you sick?" she asked. This, I thought, was precisely the right question for Ms. T to be asking. In asking it, she was reestablishing the line between her and me, and telling me that I had been destructive in blurring it.

"No, I'm not, so far as I know. But you're afraid I am." This response did not sound like me, even as I was saying it. In retrospect, I can see that I was dreaming something with this patient—a dream in which I was not myself (for either the patient or myself), and I could not find my way back to myself.

"I don't want you to brush me off by saying you're well when you're not. Tell me the truth, please. You're scaring me. Please tell me the truth." Here the patient was imploring me to speak truthfully with her about what had occurred between us.

I said, "You're telling me something that's terrifying you: the person whom you thought I was has disappeared. It seems as if someone has switched places with me. I'm someone whom you thought you could trust, but now you can't." Finally, I was being truthful with Ms. T. I sounded like myself as I spoke to her.

"Stop it. I have to leave."

I said, "I think I understand how very frightened and angry you are at me, but I hope you'll stay. You shouldn't have to be alone with what you're feeling. You've had to do that too many times in your life." Here I was asking Ms. T to allow me to continue to be her analyst, despite the fact that I had ceased being the analyst she needed earlier in the session. I was also alluding to her experience with her parents, but I did not want her to redirect toward her parents the fear and anger she was experiencing toward me in the dream we were dreaming in the session.

"Do you promise you're not sick?"

"I think you're asking me, and justifiably so, whether I had fallen ill, in the sense of losing my mind, when I told you the story that had come to me while you were talking on the phone."

"I am. ... Did you lose your mind? I didn't recognize you."

"I was not the analyst you needed when I told you what I was thinking, so it's no wonder you didn't recognize me."

After a few moments, Ms. T said in a much calmer and more businesslike cadence and tone, "I can't believe I took that phone call. It was such a rude thing to do." There was a palpable shift in the tenor of the session as the patient said these words. It felt as if the dream we had been dreaming had been abruptly interrupted in a way that reminded me of a child sweeping crayons off a table when she became too upset by what she was feeling and imagining while drawing. The dream Ms. T and I had been dreaming was one in which I had become terrifyingly unrecognizable. As a result of our

107

attempt to talk with one another as honestly as we could, the dream was evolving in a direction that I felt held the potential to allow her to simultaneously dream the events of the session and childhood events that she had not been able to experience when they were occurring.

In the session I have just described, the patient and I were not dreaming *about* the session or dreaming *of* the session or dreaming *in* the session. We were dreaming the session in a way that made the session a living dream that began in the patient's lateness to the session (which I dreamt in the form of the "notes" I took: the imminent bursting of the consulting room; the traffic? the accident?—the fear).

The dream continued when the patient arrived: the little girl with her coat mis-buttoned; the phone call out of nowhere; the reverie of the terrified, lost child—my reverie; her reverie; our reverie. My telling her the story—for my sake, in response to my feeling lost. Her speaking the truth of what had happened and demanding that I speak honestly with her about it: I had disappeared, I had frightened her, I had ceased being the analyst I had been, the analyst she needed, the analyst she deserved. And finally, Ms. T (and perhaps I, too) was not able to continue to dream together that day. Instead—in a different state, in a different tone of voice—she apologized in a way that felt submissive to me, a way of being with me that lacked the intense realness of the dream we had been dreaming.

The works

Before beginning analysis with J, a 17-year-old boy, I met once with his mother. She told me that he had gradually "become another person" in the course of the previous seven or eight months, and had become "completely disconnected from reality" during the most recent month or two. She said that he used to be a well-liked, good-hearted boy who did extremely well in school and had been a protective big brother to his younger brother, who was 12.

"Now he hardly talks and has almost nothing to do with other people. He just stays in his room and watches TV. He goes out for walks in the neighborhood, but he almost always gets lost and has to be brought home by a neighbor or the police. At home he sometimes stands frozen in the foyer, saying incomprehensible things to himself."

J's mother said that she had taken him to a psychiatrist, who gave him the diagnosis of paranoid schizophrenia and prescribed medications that he refused to take. When it came time to see the psychiatrist the following week, J refused to go. He met with two other psychiatrists, but again refused to meet with them a second time. There was a strange flatness, an absence of feeling tone to J's mother's voice as she told me about him.

On meeting J for the first time in the waiting room, I introduced myself as Dr. Ogden. J abruptly got up from his chair without looking at me and followed me into my consulting room. He was a large, bulky boy wearing a T-shirt with a Grateful Dead logo on it. On entering my office, J stepped quickly toward the armchair and sat there stiffly, but only for a moment before standing up, looking around the room, and then saying to nobody in particular, "I'll have a hamburger with the works."

I said, "I'll see what I can do with what I've got here."

"You don't have anything to eat here?"

"Mostly it's me here."

"Where's the television?"

"That's me, too."

"You're not a doctor, are you?"

"I am a doctor, but I'm not one of the doctors you've met with recently."

This conversation seemed to be taking place in the English language, but none of the words J used held their usual meanings: "hamburger," "the works," "television," "doctor." I did not know what these words meant, but nonetheless I tried to talk to him in his mad language.

J lay down on the floor, flat on his back. He was silent for a few moments before saying, "There's an alligator up there with his eyes closed." He then asked in a demanding way, "What kind of doctor are you?"

I said, "A talking doctor. I talk to people who are lost and don't know who they are."

J got to his feet and walked to the bookshelf across the room. He took a book from one of the shelves and held it in his hand, seemingly more interested in its heft and texture than in its title or contents. He was very serious about what he was doing. As I watched him, I felt the sensation on my face of being touched by a blind person as he tried to get a sense of what I look like.

J carefully put the book back on the shelf in the place from which he had taken it. There was order, as well as a suggestion of tenderness, amidst the devastation. I was surprised by the tenderness. I had half expected him to throw the book across the room.

J, still facing the bookshelf, said again, "What kind of doctor are you?" Although he was seemingly addressing me, it felt as if he were talking to someone I did not know, certainly not to me. He spoke in a bizarre tone of voice that added to the strangeness of what he said and did.

I responded, "A doctor who might be able to help you find what you're looking for."

Long silence.

"My mother's dying."

"I'm sorry to hear that."

"I can smell it," he said.

After a pause of a few moments, he said, "What do you say?"

I said, "I'm confused." I tried not to ask J questions because we were talking in different languages, and so my questions would not only be incomprehensible to him, but would also demonstrate that I did not know him at all. So instead of asking "What are you talking about?," I told him a little bit of what *I* was thinking and feeling: "I'm confused."

I also limited myself to making statements about what *I* thought, as opposed to what I thought *he* was thinking. I did so in order not to convey the impression that I knew what he was thinking, because I thought it critical to let him know that his mind was his and his alone, and I had no interest in stealing it from him or putting my own ideas into his head.

"To people who come here," he said, registering his frustration with my slowness to understand his question, "what do you say?"

I said, "I'm talking with you now, so I say whatever I've been saying to you." What a poor reply, I thought, as I heard the words come from my mouth. It felt to me as if we were talking *at* one another, hoping that something, anything, would "stick," would be comprehensible to the other. I did not know what was happening, other than that J and I were lost to one another. We both were lost, but it seemed to me that we were in the very early stages of dreaming the experience of being lost.

Now, turning from the bookshelf to look me in the eye for the first time, J yelled at me, "*Who are you?*"

After a brief pause, I said, "J, I'm a person who wants to try to talk with you."

I do not usually use a patient's name when we talk. On hearing myself say the word *J*, I felt that *J* no longer felt like the patient's name. *J* now felt to me as if it were just a sound, not a name. I felt as if a chain reaction had been set in motion that had the power to destroy anything in its path. It seemed quite possible that J (and I) were in the process of experiencing a breakdown of the fragile psychic structure that he was able to maintain some of the time.

He sat down, and in a soft, pseudo-conciliatory tone of voice that barely masked his anger, said, "Who?"

I did not know what he was asking. I had again forgotten the question. I said, "I'm lost again."

He stared at me and said gruffly and a bit menacingly, "Who are you?"

I said, "I'm someone who might be able to help *you* come to know who *you* are"—a statement that felt hollow to me.

He stood, looked at the ceiling, and in a very agitated state, shouted, "*Who are you!*" He then stood rigidly with his face turned to the ceiling in a way that seemed to be stretching the muscles and tendons in his neck with such violent force that they were in danger of being torn.

I said firmly and calmly, "J, I told you I'm a doctor who talks. I don't *do* things, I never do violent things, and I ask that of you. I think you're showing me that everything that holds you together and makes you who you are is being ripped apart. I won't let that happen here." It seemed to me at this moment that J was showing me he was in a life-and-death battle with a mother/me inside of him who both held him together and tore him apart.

He remained silent, maintaining the same fixed position for a minute or so before bending his knees and lowering himself to the floor, where he lay on his back, once again looking at the ceiling. The room smelled to me like the over-oxygenated air that had been used to remove the odor of smoke from my consulting room after there had been a fire in the building a few months earlier.

I said, "I can't and won't tell you who you are, but I think I can help *you* do that." This finally felt to me to be the right way to put what I had been feeling and had been trying to say.

J said, "Oh" in a tone that was not bizarre—a human tone of voice, which conveyed a feeling that he understood what I had said.

111

An unusual thought occurred to me in the silence that followed. His saying "Oh" seemed to me to be his reticent way of saying my name by using its first letter, O. I did not know whether this was simply a wish on my part, born of the intense isolation I was feeling, or part of the dream that J and I were dreaming. Probably it was both, I thought.

Handing the baby to the mother

Ms. V's sessions had become tightly focused on solving ("figuring out") problems she was having with friends, with her supervisor at work, with relatives. It had felt to me for some time that we were going over the same ground again and again without the slightest hint of change. Ms. V seemed incapable of engaging with me in a way that felt real and alive. She and I had been working together for three years at this point.

During one of the sessions in this period of the analysis, I found myself looking at the clock frequently to see how much more time there was in the session. The hands of the clock did not seem to move. I wondered if the battery had died. Imagining replacing the batteries of the clock, I could smell the metallic odor of the metal prongs holding the battery between them; I could feel the sensation in my fingers as they pressed the dead battery to one end against the tiny spring—getting my finger under the battery, lifting it out, and tossing it into the wastepaper basket. A vivid, very disturbing set of visual images then came to mind in which I was delivering the still-born baby of a heartbroken, childless mother and throwing it into a stainless steel pan.

The analysis took on a sudden and unexpected intensity when Ms. V's dog fell ill to a serious disease. It was only then that it became fully real to me that the most intense love Ms. V had been able to feel in her adult life was the love she felt for her dog, now 14 years old. He was very ill, had no appetite, and his legs could hardly support him. Ms. V fed him water with a medicine dropper. She told me in detail about the herbal remedies that she added to the water she was feeding her dog. (She never once mentioned his name.) Ms. V was getting little sleep and spent hours in the middle of the night combing the Internet for possible cures for her dog's illness.

The patient and I met five times each week, and I invited her to call me over the weekends if she wanted to talk, but she never called.

I worried that Ms. V might sink into an incapacitating depression, as she had done twice before in adult life—at 26, after her mother's death, and at 35, after her grandfather's death.

These depressions, I thought, were failed attempts at grieving the loss of her sister, older by three years, who had "disappeared" when the patient was five. Ms. V had "adored and worshipped" her sister (whose name she never told me). One day her sister was gone, without a single word spoken by her parents about it; they acted as if nothing had changed. The patient knew that she was not to ask where her sister was. Only in her teens did she learn from an aunt that her sister had been hospitalized and died of acute leukemia.

In a previous analysis, the fact that Ms. V's sister's absence was not acknowledged by her parents "never came up." I had inquired about the patient's sister early on, when the patient was being unusually vague about the circumstances of her death. We had talked a good deal about the patient's detachment from the experience of the loss of her sister, both as a child and as an adult. I knew that it was critical that I not act as if nothing was happening.

In one of our sessions, I said to Ms. V, "I think that you're trying to save both your dog and your sister." She agreed, with little emotion in her voice.

During her sessions, Ms. V became increasingly silent as she lay limply on the couch. As time went on, I became increasingly alarmed. I said to her, "It feels to me that you're disappearing in your silence as your sister disappeared. You're even disappearing physically as you lose more and more weight." Ms. V's clothes hung limply on her now, due to the weight she had lost in the course of the previous months. I felt that I was being conscripted into the role of helpless observer of the patient's disappearance, which was inseparable from her sister's disappearance and the patient's fear of her dog's disappearance. The patient was determined to defeat death/disappearance.

As I sat in silence with Ms. V during a session in this part of the analysis, an elderly friend came to mind, a man who was one of the few obstetricians of his time to ask the mothers of stillborn babies if they wanted to hold the dead infant. He told me that not a single mother had said no. It seemed to me that Ms. V's yet-to-be-experienced grieving of her sister's death was the stillborn infant I was unconsciously being asked to deliver.

113

I said to Ms. V, "I worry that in trying to save your dog's life, you're going to miss out on—and your dog will miss out on—your being with him and keeping him company as he dies, and letting him feel your love for him and the pain you feel while he's dying."

Ms. V wept as she said, "I don't want that to happen."

I said, "I know you don't." My thought of my friend who handed the stillborn baby to the mother felt like the resumption of dreaming the session with Ms. V. Dreaming the analytic session had begun with the reverie in which I removed (delivered) and threw away the dead battery/baby from the clock whose hands had stopped moving. Aspects of that reverie were now coming to life in a new form, one in which the stillborn baby (the patient's yet-to-be-experienced grief) was being given over to the patient to hold, to feel, and to grieve.

Ms. V began our next meeting, a Monday session, by saying in a voice so choked with tears that she could get out only a few words at a time, "My dog died over the weekend. He died while I was lying down on the floor of the living room and he was on my chest. We lay there for hours. I dozed some of the time. I knew when he died."

First there was deadness: the deadness of time, interminable time, time that passed for time, but in fact was time that did not pass, because there was no past, no history, no death. Instead there was a void: the absence in the patient, the absence of the patient. We were able to begin to dream the session—the dream of the petrified hands of the clock, the dead batteries tossed away. Desperate attempts at magic—medicine-dropper feedings, herbal remedies, Internet cures—gave way to dreaming the doctor who could hold the stillborn baby and hand it to the mother, and to the patient's experience of holding her dog/sister on her chest as he/she died and did not disappear.

Conclusion

Dreaming the analytic session is an experience created by patient and analyst. At times, the patient or the analyst seems to be the dreamer, but this impression is illusory. Neither patient nor analyst alone (and no two other people) has the capacity to dream the undreamt or interrupted dreams that the patient brings to his or her analysis. These dreams are the dreams of the unconscious analytic third created by patient and analyst and experienced separately by patient and analyst. The word *psychoanalysis* is a plural noun: there are no two analyses that are alike.

I have offered three illustrations of dreaming the session. Each analyst must find with his patient a way of dreaming a session that is unique to the two of them. Adopting a "technique" prevents such a process from occurring, for it renders the session impersonal, generic. Dreaming the session is not something one works at; rather, one tries not to get in its way.

References

Bion, W. R. (1962a). *Learning from Experience*. London: Tavistock.

Bion, W. R. (1962b). A theory of thinking. In *Second Thoughts*. New York: Jason Aronson, 1967, pp. 110–119.

Bion, W. R. (1967). Notes on the theory of schizophrenia. In *Second Thoughts*. New York: Aronson, pp. 23–35.

Bion, W. R. (1970). *Attention and Interpretation*. London: Tavistock.

Bion, W. R. (1987). Clinical seminars. In *Clinical Seminars and Other Works*, edited by F. Bion. London: Karnac, pp. 1–240.

Bion, W. R. (1992). *Cogitations*, ed. F. Bion. London: Karnac.

Civitarese, G. (2013). Bion's "evidence" and his theoretical style. *The Psychoanalytic Quarterly*, 82:615–633.

Freud, S. (1900). *The Interpretation of Dreams*. SE, 4/5.

Freud, S. (1923). Two encyclopaedia articles. SE, 18.

Grotstein, J. (2000). *Who Is the Dreamer Who Dreams the Dream? A Study of Psychic Presences*. Hillsdale, NJ: Analytic Press.

Ogden, T. H. (1989). On the concept of the autistic-contiguous position. *The International Journal of Psychoanalysis*, 70:127–140.

Ogden, T. H. (1994). The analytic third—working with intersubjective clinical facts. *The International Journal of Psychoanalysis*, 73:3–20.

Ogden, T. H. (1997). Reverie and interpretation. *The Psychoanalytic Quarterly*, 66:567–595.

Ogden, T. H. (2003). On not being able to dream. *The International Journal of Psychoanalysis*, 84:17–30.

Ogden, T. H. (2004a). This art of psychoanalysis: dreaming undreamt dreams and interrupted cries. *The International Journal of Psychoanalysis*, 85:857–877.

Ogden, T. H. (2004b). On holding and containing, being and dreaming. *The International Journal of Psychoanalysis*, 85:1349–1364.

Ogden, T. H. (2005). *This Art of Psychoanalysis: Dreaming Undreamt Dreams and Interrupted Cries*. London: Routledge.

Ogden, T. H. (2010). On three forms of thinking: magical thinking, dream thinking, and transformative thinking. *The Psychoanalytic Quarterly*, 79: 317–347.

Ogden, T. H. (2014). Fear of breakdown and the unlived life. *The International Journal of Psychoanalysis*, 95:205–224.

Sandler, J. (1976). Dreams, unconscious phantasies, and "identity of perception." *The International Review of Psycho-Analysis*, 3:33–42.

Winnicott, D. W. (1971). Fear of breakdown. In *Psychoanalytic Explorations*, edited by C. Winnicott, R. Shepherd & M. Davis. Cambridge, MA: Harvard Univ. Press, 1989, pp. 87–95.

6

TOWARD A REVISED FORM OF ANALYTIC THINKING AND PRACTICE

The evolution of analytic theory of mind

I have come to view the work of Freud, Klein, Fairbairn, Winnicott, and Bion on the emergence of mind and the conception of mind as instrumental in the evolution of a new and generative psychoanalytic sensibility and mode of practice, as I have discussed in earlier chapters of this book. In this chapter I will trace in the work of these authors a movement from a conception of mind as a "mental apparatus" for *processing experience* (in the work of Freud, Klein, and Fairbairn) to a conception of mind as a process located in *the very act of experiencing* (in the work of Winnicott and Bion). The evolution of this strand of thinking might be thought of as a movement from a notion of mind as a noun, to a notion of mind as a verb, a living process, perpetually in the act of coming into being.

I will offer a sketch of elements of each of these analysts' theories or hypotheses or stories concerning the beginnings of psychic life. I add the term *stories* to the terms *theories* and *hypotheses* because no one, even the most devoted mother, knows what it is to be inside the psyche–soma of a newborn infant. In recent years, infant observation has afforded us an opportunity to gain a sense of the experience of mother and infant, but we can do no more than make inferences about, and metaphors concerning, the interior life of the infant. We are still in the position of a person born without eyes trying to imagine the experience of sight. The person without eyes may use his other senses, and may create metaphors for what sight may be "like," but they do not add up to the experience of seeing.

DOI: 10.4324/9781003228462-6

I find that a study of the hypotheses of each of these theorists concerning the emergence of mind creates another vantage point from which to view each theorist's broader conception of the way the mind works in later stages of life, which, in turn, sheds light on what it is to be human.

Each of the theorists has more than one version of genesis, so my rendering of their ideas necessarily tells one version of their stories of "the beginning," which in a sense makes me the storyteller for each of them. Moreover, I will along the way offer my own interpretations and extensions of the ideas under discussion, some of which I believe are implicit in the work of each author, while others entail my own elaboration of his or her work.

In writing this chapter over the course of several years, I began with the hypothesis that the stories of the emergence of mind of each of the five theorists could be stated in the form of a response to the question: What is the problem for which the emergence of mind is a solution? This proved to be useful in relation to the work of Freud, Klein, and Fairbairn, but not for the conceptions of the emergence of mind and the concept of mind in the work of Winnicott and Bion. This brought to my awareness a radical change in analytic thinking that has its roots in the work of Freud, Klein, and Fairbairn and came to fruition in the work of Winnicott and Bion. It is the evolution of this change in analytic thinking that is the focus of this chapter.

Freud

Freud's conception of the birth of the mind is something of a collage he created over the course of more than four decades. The pieces of the collage were not assembled in chronological order. In fact, Freud's conception of the earliest state of the psyche, which he called the "oceanic feeling" (1929, p. 54), is an idea and a term presented to him by his friend, Romain Rolland, in a letter written in 1927.

Freud (1929), in *Civilization and Its Discontents*, adopted the term *oceanic feeling* to describe the earliest psychic state: "[the oceanic feeling] is a feeling of an indissoluble bond, of being one with the external world as a whole" (p. 65).

While the ego becomes more differentiated from the external world, it retains "a residue" of the oceanic feeling as a background state:

..., originally the ego includes everything, later it separates off an external world from itself. Our present ego-feeling is, therefore, only a shrunken residue of a much more inclusive—indeed, an all-embracing—feeling which corresponded to a more intimate bond between the ego and the world about it. ... the same ideas with which my friend elucidated the "oceanic" feeling.

(1929, p. 68)

Freud (1929) uses the term "the ego" (p. 67) (*das Ich*, better translated as "the I") here, but does not offer a definition of the term. Instead, by means of quite extraordinary use of language, he indirectly conveys transformations of "I-ness" (subjectivity) as they occur in development subsequent to the "all-embracing" "oceanic" feeling–state.

An infant at the breast does not as yet distinguish his ego from the external world as the source of the sensations flowing in upon him. He gradually learns to do so, in response to various promptings. He must be very strongly impressed by the fact that some sources of excitation, which he will later recognize as his own bodily organs, can provide him with sensations at any moment, whereas other sources evade him from time to time—among them what he desires most of all, his mother's breast—and only reappear as a result of his screaming for help. In this way there is for the first time set over against the ego an "object," in the form of something which exists "outside" and which is only forced to appear by a special action.

(1929, pp. 66–67)

Here, Freud is describing the birth of the subject. With the "birth" of the object ("something which exists 'outside'"), there is in that same moment the birth of the subject: there can be no separate object ("not-I") in the absence of a subject ("I") to experience it; and there can be no subject ("I") without an object to encounter that is experienced as "not-I."

In developing a conception of the next "step" in, or aspect of, the emergence of mind, Freud picks up a line of thought that he introduced almost 20 years earlier in "Formulations on two principles of mental functioning" (1911a): the idea that the ego is unable to successfully attain pleasure or avert pain by "hallucinati[ng] the

119

fulfillment of its internal needs" (pp. 219–220). For example, when operating solely on the basis of the pleasure principle, wishful hallucinations of food will not satisfy hunger. This is the impetus for the ego to begin to operate both on the basis of the "reality principle" (Freud, 1911a) and "the pleasure principle" (1911a), and to enter into object-relationships with real external objects:

> A further incentive to a disengagement of the ego from the general mass of sensations—that is, to the recognition of an "outside," an external world—is provided by the frequent, manifold and unavoidable sensations of pain and unpleasure ... One comes to learn a procedure by which, through a deliberate action, one can differentiate between what is internal—what belongs to the ego—and what is external—what emanates from the outer world.
>
> (1929, p. 67)

As is reflected in the passages I have just quoted, it is in the medium of bodily sensation that the ego (the I) comes into being: "The ego is first and foremost a bodily ego" (Freud, 1923, p. 26).

The foregoing set of ideas concerning what, for Freud, are the earliest states of mind, serve as the background for his conception of the formation and elaboration of the conscious and unconscious mind. The primordial mind is faced with the problem of dealing with the disturbing effects of instinctual pressure emanating from the body: instinct, for Freud, "is the demand [of the body] made upon the mind for work" (Freud, 1915a, p. 122). The inception of that "mental apparatus" (Freud, 1900) takes the form of the development of the capacity to create "psychical representative[s]" (p. 1915a, p.122) of instinct (at first, primarily the sexual instinct [Freud, 1905]). In other words, mind is a structure, a "mental apparatus," for processing instinct-derived bodily experience by creating psychic representations of that experience.

The psychical representatives and derivatives of the sexual instinct (thoughts, feelings, phantasies, and impulses) that are created generate problems of their own, namely the fact that many of the phantasies and impulses generated are unacceptable, frightening, shameful, terrifying, overwhelming, and so on. This emotional problem is met by the creation of a divide in human consciousness that separates and connects the unconscious and conscious–preconscious aspects of mind. The concept of the dynamic unconscious mind necessarily involves a conception of the unconscious and conscious mind operating according to different principles (the "pleasure principle" and the "reality principle," respectively [Freud, 1911a]). Neither the idea of the unconscious mind nor the idea of the conscious mind has any meaning in isolation from the other: each creates, maintains, and negates the other (Ogden, 1992a). This may be Freud's most important contribution to the development of a general psychology: "If Freud's discovery had to be summed up in a single word, that word without doubt would have to be 'unconscious'" (Laplanche and Pontalis, 1973, p. 474).

Intrinsic to Freud's conception of the conscious and unconscious mind is his concept of repression: "The theory of repression is the corner-stone on which the whole structure of psycho-analysis rests" (Freud, 1911b, p. 16). Repression is the psychic function that creates and preserves the separation of, and the communication between, the conscious-preconscious and the unconscious aspects of mind. Without repression, there is no unconscious (or conscious) mind. Thus, the creation of mind, for Freud, is the "solution" to the problem, beginning in early infancy, of powerful animal instincts (particularly the sexual instinct) that are so disturbing that a "mental apparatus" must be developed in order to cope with the psychic representations of the sexual instinct.

At this point in the discussion of Freud's view of the creation of mind, I will interject something of my own interpretation of his writings. The mental apparatus that is created in response to instinctual pressure protects us from ourselves (our frightening, unacceptable impulses and phantasies), while at the same time *safeguarding banished parts of ourselves*. Repression sends into exile aspects of ourselves while keeping those same aspects close to us, never completely silenced, continually reminding us of the disowned aspects of who we are, and who we are afraid we are. In effect, we are "burying ourselves *alive*" in the repressed unconscious, and those buried aspects of self are continually "banging on the door" of the repression barrier (the ever-present threat [and promise] of the "*return of the repressed*" [Freud, 1915b, p. 154, original emphasis]).

The work of repression, so conceived, is that of creating and preserving a form of divided, yet unitary, consciousness in which we disown aspects of ourselves, and relegate them to a domain (the unconscious) which, like the figures outside the cave in Plato's allegory, are "perceived" only as shadows, reflections. The psycho-analytic unconscious is a mysterious aspect of ourselves—never fully understandable, making itself "known" only as "reflected" in deriv-ative forms such as dreams, symptoms, slips of the tongue, artistic creations, and so on.

By means of our dual consciousness, it *seems* that we "get to have it both ways"—a coexistence of the feared and the embraced, which stand in dialectical tension with one another. But, to my mind, it is not quite accurate to say that we succeed in having it both ways because, by the use of repression, we figuratively *bury ourselves alive*. Repression, while preserving unconsciously what is *too much of ourselves* for us to bear, also depletes us by cutting us off from ourselves. We become less fully ourselves. From this perspec-tive, I would say that the effort to help a patient restore himself to himself is the therapeutic goal of psychoanalysis. While Freud (1900) most often articulated the goal of psychoanalysis as that of making the unconscious conscious (and available to secondary process thinking), I would restate this conception in the following way: the therapeutic aim of psychoanalysis is the "safe return" to the patient of aspects of himself that have been buried alive and are not yet dead.

Klein

If, for Freud, the psychic world begins with a whimper—"an indis-soluble bond, of being one with the external world as a whole"—the creation of mind, for Klein, begins with a bang. "The ego exists and operates from birth onwards" (Klein, 1963, p. 300) and immediately faces a pressing emotional problem.

Klein's understanding of the nature of the problem with which the ego must contend "*ab initio*" (Klein, 1952a, p. 57) stands in stark contrast with Freud's (1905, 1940) understanding of the earliest anxieties, those involving the psychic representatives of the sexual instinct, which, for him, do not come into play at the very outset of life.

Klein (1952a) states,

> I differ, however, from Freud in that I put forward the hypoth-esis that the primary cause of anxiety is the fear of annihilation,

of death, arising from the work of the death instinct within. ...
The primordial fear of being annihilated forces the ego into
action and engenders the first defences.

(p. 57)

The earliest emotional problem faced by the infant, from Klein's
perspective, derives from the workings of the death instinct. And the
earliest development of the mind occurs as the ego is forced "into
action" in response to the anxieties elicited by the death instinct.
The "action" taken by the primordial ego is that of creating "unconscious phantasies" (1952a), which are "pre-verbal" in nature and are
"felt by the infant in much more primitive ways than language can
express" (Klein, 1957, p. 180, fn. 1). For instance, phantasy is the
form in which meaning is attributed to the conflict between, on the
one hand, "extreme and powerful" (Klein, 1952b, p. 64) aggressive
feelings and impulses derived from the death instinct, and on the
other, loving ("libidinal" [Klein, 1952b, p. 62]) feelings toward the
mother derived from the life instinct.

The idea that phantasy is the ego's response to "[t]he primordial
fear of being annihilated" is a stunning contribution to the psychoanalytic concept of the emergence of mind and of the concept
of mind: phantasy is the form in which all unconscious meaning is
experienced, represented, and structured.

The inner world of the infant—the unconscious mind—is the
world of object-related phantasy. In other words, the entirety of the
unconscious mind takes the form of phantasied internal object relationships (Klein, 1934). For example, the feeling of envy, "the earliest direct externalization of the death instinct" (Segal, 1964, p. 40),
exists in the inner world as a phantasied relationship between internal objects. Envy is a principal emotional tie between the infant and
the "feeding breast ... [which in the infant's phantasies] possesses
everything he desires and ... has an unlimited flow of milk, and
love which the breast keeps for its own gratification" (Klein, 1957,
p. 183). However, this "solution" (the creation of a narrative structure experienced in the form of unconscious phantasy) generates a
problem of its own. The fact that the breast is also the source of the
infant's life-sustaining milk and love makes it a perilous object to
attack in phantasy. The ego must then take further defensive action
in the form of a phantasied splitting of the breast into a good breast

and a bad breast. This allows the infant to safely love the good breast and safely hate the bad breast. Thus, the defenses, too, are object-related phantasies (Isaacs, 1952; Klein, 1957).

Phantasying—the infant's principal "solution" to the problem posed by the earliest anxieties—represents a revolutionary trans-formation of Freud's conception of the unconscious. Klein posits that from the very beginning of life, there is a differentiation of the conscious and unconscious mind in which unconscious phantasy constitutes the entirety of its content and structure, which in turn powerfully affects the development of both one's thinking and one's ways of relating to external objects:

> …, phantasies and feelings about the state of the internal object vitally influence the structure of the ego. …
>
> *It is in phantasy that the infant splits the object and the self, but the effect of this phantasy is a very real one, because it leads to feelings and relations (and later on, thought processes) being in fact cut off from one another.*
>
> (Klein, 1946, p. 6, emphasis added)

From the beginning of psychic life, splitting of self and object occur *in phantasy*, but the effects *of phantasy* are "very real" in that they lead to internal and external object relations "being in fact cut off from one another." In terms of the inner world, the unconscious becomes altered in its very structure as sets of object relationships are cut off from other sets of object relationships in phantasy. "[A]nd later on," not only do internal and external object relations become discon-nected emotionally, the different aspects of thinking ("thought pro-cesses") are "being in fact cut off from one another." If, for example, primary and secondary process thinking are "disconnected" from one another, playing, dreaming, learning, and creative thinking become severely limited or are extinguished altogether. In addition, the integrity of the ego (the sense of who one is, I would add) is very difficult to maintain. Klein (1955), in her paper "On identification," describes the depletion and ultimately the death of the psyche when projective identification is excessive.

A fundamental part of Klein's (1958) conception of the emergence of mind, which occurs at birth, is her belief that how one fares psy-chically as an infant is, to a large degree, determined by the inborn strength of death instinct relative to life instinct.

> The strength of the ego—reflecting the state of fusion between the two instincts—is, I believe, constitutionally determined. If in the fusion the life instinct predominates, which implies an ascendency of the capacity for love, the ego is relatively strong, and is more able to bear the anxiety arising from the death instinct and to counteract it.
>
> (1958, pp. 238–239)

Of course, the reverse is also true: if the death instinct is stronger than the life instinct, the ego is relatively weak and less able "to bear the anxiety arising from the death instinct and to counteract it," and consequently prone to the development of pathological defensive mental structures or fragmentation of mental structure.

Klein's idea that the unconscious is structured by phantasy is quite different from Freud's (1923) structural model, which conceives of the mind as structured by the id, ego, and superego, a metaphorical committee in which the ego attempts to manage the impulsive aspect of self (the id), and the judgmental aspect of self (the superego), in its efforts to deal realistically with external reality and thereby derive maximal pleasure and satisfaction from life in the real external world. Klein continues to use the term "ego," but it has a meaning quite different from Freud's use of the term. In Klein's work, the ego ("the I") that is present from birth onward is both the creator of unconscious phantasy and a figure in those phantasies— phantasies that are both psychic representatives of the death instinct and defenses generated in response to fears of annihilation "arising from the work of the death instinct."

Fairbairn

Fairbairn's conception of the birth of the mind is as radically different from Klein's as Klein's is different from Freud's. For Fairbairn, the most difficult emotional problem the infant faces at the beginning of life, and the impetus for the creation of the unconscious and conscious mind, is the infant's experience of his mother as both loving and unloving ("unsatisfactory" [Fairbairn, 1940, p. 13]). This "problem" is better called a "catastrophe" because the infant's psychic and physical survival depends upon his ability to cope with it. This emotional crisis is a universal aspect of the early relationship with the (real) mother, but differs greatly in intensity depending on constitutional factors and the quality of the mother's care of the infant (Fairbairn, 1940, 1944). Fairbairn's placing the relationship with the real mother at the core of the creation of mind and the preservation of the sanity and the physical life of the individual beginning at birth was, at the time he published these papers, nothing short of a transformative contribution to the psychoanalytic conception of the creation of the conscious and unconscious mind.

For Fairbairn (1944), the infant's experience of feeling unlovable by his actual mother engenders in him feelings of "shame" (1940, p. 113), "worthlessness" (p. 113), "beggardom" (p. 113), and "impotence" (p. 113). And

> At a still deeper level (or at a still earlier stage) the child's experience is one of, so to speak, exploding ineffectively and being completely emptied of libido [love]. It is thus an experience of disintegration and of imminent psychical death. …
> [In being] threatened with loss of his libido (which for him constitutes his own goodness) and ultimately with the loss of the ego structure that constitutes himself.
>
> (Fairbairn, 1944, p. 113)

It should be noted that Fairbairn uses the term "ego" (which "is present from birth" [Fairbairn, 1963, p. 224]) to refer not only to the entirety of the conscious and unconscious mind, but also to the personality as a whole ("himself"), including the subjective states of the individual.

From Fairbairn's perspective, the infant's psychic response to feeling unlovable is the emergence of a mind created by "internalizing" the unsatisfactory part of the relationship with the mother. The word *internalizing* is invented anew by Fairbairn here (just as Freud reinvented the word *unconscious* and Klein reinvented the word *phantasy*). No longer is internalization an introjective phantasy, as it is for Klein and Freud. When Fairbairn uses the concept of internalization in relation to the early unsatisfactory aspect of the relationship with the mother, he is referring to structural change of the infant's mind. Parts of the "ego," which to my mind is synonymous with self in Fairbairn's work, are split off from the main body of the ego/self and repressed. These repressed *parts of the ego/self* enter into *actual* (not phantasied) internal object relationships with one another in a way that replicates aspects of the unsatisfactory relationship with the real external object mother. Internal objects are real, not phantasied, in the sense that they each are, in themselves, capable of thinking, feeling, and relating as they interact with other aspects of the ego/ self (Fairbairn, 1944; see also Ogden, 2010).

The internalization of the unsatisfactory aspect of the relationship with the mother is the impetus for the creation and structuring of the unconscious mind. With the formation of an unconscious mind, there is, by definition, the formation of a conscious mind and a repression barrier that regulates movement of emotional content (thoughts and feelings) between the two. Fairbairn (1940, 1944) views repression as an unconscious ego function that is an expression of the infant's anger at the unsatisfactory mother for reducing him to "beggardom" (Fairbairn, 1944, p. 113) and "impotence" (p. 113).

For Fairbairn (1944), the repressed unconscious mind created in this way is structured in the form of paired addictive internal object relationships between (1) an aspect of the ego/self endlessly craving the love of an exciting internal object that will never return that love; and (2) an aspect of the ego endlessly trying to win the love of a rejecting internal object.

This internal object world is a "closed system" (Fairbairn, 1958, p. 385) in which, it seems to me, the principal driving force is the insatiable (futile) effort to change the bad (tantalizing and rejecting) internal objects into good (loving) ones (Ogden, 2010). The only exit from this closed system is the redirection of libidinal ties from internal objects (split-off parts of the ego/self) to real external objects. This conversion of addictive ties to internal objects to loving ties with real external objects is the final, yet never to be completed, step in the formation of the healthy conscious mind (which is engaged in relating to and internalizing the admired and beloved aspects of real external objects) and the unconscious mind (which is taken up with addictive ties between internal objects). This conception of the mind is reflected in Fairbairn's (1958) clinical technique. For instance, he rejected the use of the couch and instead sat behind his desk while the patient sat in a chair faced slightly away from Fairbairn (the real object always being within view, if the patient desires).

In summary, Fairbairn introduced a radical shift in the conception of the emergence of mind. From Klein's perspective, and to a lesser extent, from Freud's, the pressure of instinct (the death instinct and the sexual instinct, respectively) presents the infant early on with "a problem" that forces the ego "into action" (Klein, 1952a, p. 57), that is, the elaboration of a conscious and unconscious mind, and the creation of a structure for each. By stark contrast, Fairbairn conceived of "the problem" faced by the infant as the threat of psychical death as a consequence of his experience of the unloving aspect of the external object mother. The "solution" to the problem is the formation of an unconscious inner world structured by addictive ties between split-off aspects of the ego/self.

Winnicott

Moving from an exploration of psychic genesis from the perspectives of Freud, Klein, and Fairbairn, to Winnicott's ideas on this subject, feels to me as if I am entering an entirely new domain. As I have discussed in the first chapter of this book, Winnicott introduced revolutionary change to psychoanalysis not simply by reconceptualizing psychic origins, but by introducing a form of analytic thinking ("ontological thinking") which had been an aspect of psychoanalytic theory and practice, but never elaborated, described, and practiced as Winnicott does.

In studying Winnicott's (1949) conception of the earliest life of the infant, we are immediately met with a paradox: "the paradox that mind does not exist as an entity" (p. 243). For Winnicott, the entity that exists from the outset is the psyche–soma, in which psyche and soma are inseparable parts of the whole.

> The mind does not exist as an entity in the individual's scheme of things provided the individual psyche–soma or body scheme has come satisfactorily through the very early developmental stages; mind is then no more than a special case of the functioning of the psyche–soma.
>
> (1949, p. 244)

When the mother is "tantalizing" (Winnicott, 1949, p. 246), the infant may develop a form of

> *mental functioning becoming a thing in itself,* practically replacing the good mother and making her unnecessary. ... [T]he psyche of the individual gets "seduced" away into this mind from the

intimate relationship which the psyche originally had with the soma. The result is a mind-psyche, which is pathological.

(pp. 246–247, original emphasis)

So, the question of the creation of "mind" in Winnicott's work must be rethought since "mind" (the "mind-psyche") is a pathological entity. The psyche-soma is primary: it is the innate condition of the infant at birth (in the care of the environmental mother).

In developing his ideas regarding the relationship of psyche and soma, Winnicott (1949) makes what for me is an astounding statement about the psyche-soma and the origins of the experience of self:

> Here is a body, and the psyche and the soma are not to be distinguished except according to the direction from which one is looking. One can look at the developing mind or at the developing psyche. I suppose the word psyche here means the *imaginative elaboration of somatic parts, feelings, and functions,* that is, of physical aliveness.
>
> (p. 244, original emphasis)

I am always taken by surprise by the last words of this passage. I expect the words to be "psychic aliveness," not "physical aliveness." But that is precisely the point Winnicott is making. "The word psyche here means" imaginatively elaborating the parts and feelings and functions of the soma. And, I would add, conversely: I suppose the word soma means, here, bestowing physicality to the psychic functions of thinking, feeling, playing, imagining, and fantasying, that is, of somatic aliveness. This, I think, is what Winnicott means when he says, "psyche and soma are not to be distinguished except according to the direction from which one is looking."

Winnicott is conceiving of psyche and soma in a way that is new to analytic thinking. He is defining them not as nouns, but as verbs. Psyche is no longer a mental apparatus, an intermediary for processing lived experience. Psyche, for Winnicott, *is* the experience of imaginatively elaborating the soma, thus creating physical aliveness. And looking at the psyche-soma from the other "direction," soma *is* the experience of bestowing physicality to psychic experience, thus creating psychic aliveness. The psyche is no longer the defensive response to bodily (instinctual) pressures (Freud and Klein) or to the unsatisfactory relationship with the mother (Fairbairn); rather, the psyche, "at the beginning" (Winnicott, 1949, p. 244), is the very act of *imaginatively elaborating* the soma, thus creating "physical aliveness."

Winnicott is reinventing the word *aliveness*, as Freud reinvented the word *unconscious*, as Klein reinvented the word *phantasy*, and as Fairbairn reinvented the word *internalization*. The creation of the combined experience of physical aliveness and psychic aliveness is the defining feature of the birth of the psyche-soma (a birth that can only occur in an "environment ... which *actively adapts* to the needs of the newly formed psyche-soma" [1949, p. 245, original emphasis]).

For Winnicott, the essential backdrop to everything the infant experiences (including the achievement of psychic and somatic aliveness) is the role of the real mother. Even before the infant is born, the mother enters into a state of "primary maternal preoccupation" (Winnicott, 1956), a state of being in which she is, to a very large extent, no longer a person separate from the baby, "the infant ... is part of herself" (Winnicott, 1971a, p. 12). Under any other circumstances the mother's state of being as she prepares for the infant's birth, and in the early days after his birth, would be considered "an illness" (1956, p. 302). Once the infant is born, the mother, in this state, "can ... feel herself into her infant's place" (1956, p. 304), in such a way that the infant is able to experience an undisrupted state of "going-on-being" (Winnicott, 1949, p. 245) (a subjectless phrase that reflects the infant's experience of being alive, while not yet being a subject). This is where *the experience of aliveness* begins.

Implicit in the discussion of Winnicott's work is the idea that the birth of the infant is not synonymous with the infant's becoming alive. Winnicott's ideas concerning psychic and somatic aliveness were introduced in his 1949 paper, "Mind and its relation to the psyche-soma." Four years later, he published what is to my mind his single most important paper, "Transitional objects and transitional phenomena." In that paper (first published in 1953 and amended in 1971), he not only elaborated the idea of the primacy of the quality of aliveness in human experience, he introduced new concepts, language, and a way of thinking about human experience that simply had not previously existed in psychoanalysis (though Winnicott would be the first to say he could not have developed his own ideas in the absence of the analytic thinking that preceded him). He did so in what seems to me a quiet sort of way.

In his "transitional object" paper (Winnicott, 1971a), he introduces the idea of "an intermediate area" of experiencing:

> From birth ... the human being is concerned with the problem of the relationship between what is objectively perceived and what is subjectively conceived of, and in the solution to this problem there is no health for the human being who has not been started off well enough by the mother. *The intermediate area to which I am referring is the area that is allowed to the infant between primary creativity* [the infant's experiencing the object as if he had created it in a way that is just right] *and objective perception based on reality-testing* [the infant's experiencing the object as a discovery]. The transitional phenomena represent the early stages of the use of illusion, without which there is no meaning for the human being in the idea of a relationship with an object that is perceived by others as external to that being.
>
> (p. 11, original emphasis)

Without a capacity for generating this intermediate area of experiencing, "there is no meaning for the human being ... in relationship with ... [the] external [object world]." So, one might say, there is a second beginning of psychic and bodily aliveness (the first occurs in the state of subjectless going-on-being). As the infant enters into the intermediate area of experiencing, he begins to experience the world as both (and neither) created and discovered, as "alive and real" (Winnicott, 1971a, p. 9). The intermediate area of transitional phenomena, "that exists (but cannot exist)" (Winnicott, 1971b, p. 107) is an area of paradox in which the object is not an internal object and not an external object, "never under magical control like the internal object nor outside control as the mother is" (Winnicott, 1971a, p. 10); it is neither "conceived of" by the infant, nor "presented to" him (p. 12) from the outside world. And the infant is and is not a subject separate from objects seen by observers to be external to the infant. These paradoxes must be "accepted and tolerated and respected" (1971c, p. xii) and not resolved, "for the price of this [resolution] is the loss of the value of the paradox itself" (p. xii).

The state of being generated in the intermediate area is the inception of what "is *felt by the individual* to form the core for the imaginative self" (Winnicott, 1949, p. 244, original emphasis), the beginnings of "the place where we live" (Winnicott, 1971b, p. 104), the place where we genuinely come to life in a way that has "all the sense of real" (Winnicott, 1963, p. 184).

The questions I have been asking of Freud, Klein, and Fairbairn concerning the birth of the mind must be rethought and reframed when approaching Winnicott. For him, the question is no longer "How does one conceive of the emergence of mind?" The question becomes "How does the infant first come to life, first come to experience physical and psychic aliveness?"

It would be an omission of an essential dimension of Winnicott's conception of the beginning of life and the inception of mind not to mention the fact that his knowledge of early life was derived, in large part, from his experience as a pediatrician, which powerfully colored his way of being with, and writing about, mothers and children, and his conception of the earliest human states of being.

In talking with an imaginary mother with her newborn, he writes,

> you must get a very funny impression of him [your baby] when he is handed to you just for you to feed him. At this time he is a bundle of discontent, a human being to be sure, but one who has raging lions and tigers inside him. And he is almost certainly scared by his own feelings. If no one has explained all this to you, you may become scared too.
>
> (1964, p. 23)

In another paper, he writes,

> A mother has to be able to tolerate hating her baby without doing anything about it. … The most remarkable thing about a mother is her ability to be hurt so much by her baby and to hate so much without paying the child out, and her ability to wait for rewards that may or may not come at a later date.
>
> (1947, p. 202)

As I quote these lines, I am reminded of something James Grotstein said to me some 30 years into our friendship. He told me that English was his second language. I was stunned. In all the time we had known one another he had never once mentioned this to me. I asked him what his first language was, and he replied, "Baby Talk."

Bion

As was the case in approaching Winnicott's work on psychic genesis and the concept of mind, I find in approaching Bion's work that I am met by radically new ways of thinking. Psychic genesis according to Bion is told in the form of two separate but inextricably interrelated accounts that differ not only in content, but also in the forms of thinking and forms of writing used to tell "the stories." It seems to me that a major shift in Bion's way of thinking began with *Elements of Psychoanalysis* (1963) and took more highly developed forms in the works that followed. The "story" I will tell is my version of Bion's story of the circumstances of the beginning of psychic life. I will try to tell the story in a way that captures the generative tension between the work of "early Bion" (pre-1963) and that of "late Bion" (1963–1979).

For "early Bion," from the very beginning of life, the infant is bombarded by raw sense impressions that are experienced as "its feeling that it is dying" (Bion, 1962a, p. 116), which I take to be a feeling of impending annihilation:

> The infant personality by itself is unable to make use of the sense-data [raw sense impressions which Bion calls beta-elements], but has to evacuate these elements into the mother, relying on her to do whatever has to be done to convert them into a form suitable for employment as alpha-elements [rudimentary thoughts that can be linked in the process of thinking and dreaming] by the infant.
>
> (Bion, 1962a, p. 116)

Bion continues,

> The mother's capacity for reverie is the receptor organ for the infant's harvest of self-sensation gained by its conscious [lived emotional experience]. ...
>
> Normal development follows if the relationship between infant and breast permits the infant to project a feeling, say, that

it is dying into the mother and to reintroject it after its sojourn in the breast has made it tolerable to the infant psyche.

(p. 116)

So, in the beginning, in a healthy mother–infant relationship, the mother's "capacity for reverie," her dreaming the infant's experience, transforms thoughts and feelings that are not yet thinkable by the infant into a form that his rudimentary, inborn mental "apparatus" (Bion, 1962a, p. 117) is able to utilize in the process of thinking and dreaming. (Dreaming, for Bion, is synonymous with unconscious psychological work, which is our richest form of thinking.) But:

> If the projection is not accepted by the mother the infant feels that its feeling that it is dying is stripped of such meaning as it has. It therefore reintrojects, not a fear of dying made tolerable, but a nameless dread. …
>
> The rudimentary consciousness cannot carry the burden placed on it. The establishment internally of a projective-identification-rejecting-object means that instead of an understanding [internal] object the infant has a willfully misunderstanding [internal] object.
>
> (1962a, pp. 116–117)

The circumstances of the beginning of life, for "early Bion," involve two people (who are not experienced as two people) living/dreaming experiences together. It must be borne in mind that the work of the mother in a state of receptive reverie is highly demanding, and includes being inhabited by the infant's "violence of emotion" (Bion, 1962b, p. 10).

I find that Poe's (1848) description of a certain kind of thought—"unthought-like thoughts that are the souls of thoughts" (p. 80)—captures, for me, the paradoxical essence of Bion's conception of the "raw sense impressions" (the immediate, unprocessed form in which we register impressions of emotional experience). These sense impressions are "unthought-like" in that they cannot be linked in the process of thinking—they are yet to be organized raw sensory data. At the same time, they are "the souls of thought" in that they are the only direct connection with our lived experience, and as such, they are the living core (the "soul") of every thought and feeling that results from the processing of this raw data. The infant's sense impressions are all he has of the experience of being alive, and this continues to be the case throughout life.

But at the beginning, the infant is flooded with sensory data derived from his lived emotional experience: "The rudimentary consciousness cannot carry the burden placed on it," which leaves the infant no option other than to "evacuate" sense-data into the mother. The mother, in a state of actively receptive reverie, *lives with the infant* what he is unable to think/experience on his own. This experience of mother and infant living the experience together creates emotional conditions in which the raw sense-data can be altered in such a way that the infant is able to think and feel his experience for himself.

But when the mother and infant are not able to transform the infant's raw sensory data, his "unthought-like thoughts" are stripped of what meaning they had held. This experience with the mother is internalized as a part of the infant that attacks his own thinking processes.

Bion's thinking in his early work is largely characterized by a hermeneutic approach. I am using the term *hermeneutic* to refer to a method of interpretation in which a part of a text or a situation is understood in relation to the whole, and the whole is understood in relation to the part, thus moving between confusion and provisional apprehension, and ultimately achieving deeper understanding (see Ricoeur [1981] and Habermas [1971] on therapeutic psychoanalysis as a hermeneutic process). Hermeneutic interpretation is dialogic, but essentially linear in nature. Bion employs a hermeneutic method, for example, in the way he conceives of the mother and infant working/living/dreaming together in rendering unthinkable thoughts and feelings utilizable by the infant's apparatus for thinking. (The idea that the mother's role in reverie is *living an experience with the infant* is my own way of understanding what occurs in early maternal reverie, but I think it is implicit in Bion's early work.)

Bion's thinking concerning the emergence of mind in his early work holds similarities with that of Freud, Klein, and Fairbairn in that the infant's earliest thinking is the "solution" (Bion, 1962b, p. 80) to a problem. For Bion, the problem to be solved is unthinkable thoughts: from the beginning "thinking has to be called into existence to cope with [unthinkable] thoughts" (Bion, 1962a, p. 29).

The theory of emergence of mind in "late Bion" is quite different from, though not contradictory with, the ideas in his early work. "Late Bion" is a thinker concerned most fundamentally with matters pertaining to *being and becoming in the present moment*, as opposed to matters of *knowing and understanding*. His paper "Notes on memory and desire" (1967) is something of a manifesto on this topic. He instructs the psychoanalyst:

Obey the following rules:

1. *Memory*: Do not remember past meetings. ...
2. *Desires*: Desires for results, "cures," or even understandings must not be allowed to proliferate [in the analyst's mind]. (1967, p. 137)

And, later in that paper:

> The psychoanalyst should aim at achieving a state of mind so that at every session he feels he has not seen the patient before. If he feels he has, he is treating the wrong patient.
>
> (p. 138)

Our reflexive wish to relive the past (perhaps in order to "get it right" this time) or to imagine ourselves in the future (which is based on the omnipotent fantasy that we have the power to predict and control what will happen) removes us from the reality of the present moment, the only moment in which the individual (the patient, the analyst, the infant) *is*, and is *coming into being*.

> The belief that reality is or could be known is mistaken because reality is not something which lends itself to being known. It is impossible to know reality for the same reason that makes it impossible to sing potatoes; they may be grown, or pulled, or eaten, but not sung. Reality has to be "been": there should be a transitive verb "to be" expressly for use with the term "reality."
>
> (Bion, 1965, p. 148)

The writing itself in this passage creates, for the reader, an opportunity to experience being alive to ideas, humor, and creativity in the experience of reading. If it is to be a real experience of reading, the reader must *become the reality* of reading this piece of writing.

Education, psychoanalysis, parenting are too often exercises in getting to know, as opposed to experiences of, *becoming* the reality of reading or of "'being' what is 'real'" (Bion, 1965, p. 148) in the analytic session.

In other words, for "late Bion," becoming alive (and this includes becoming alive to one's experience at birth) is the act of *becoming* the reality of the moment one is living in such a way that it is as unencumbered as possible by what one thinks will happen or what one wishes were happening, for those wishes dull the senses, kill the aliveness and realness of what is occurring in that moment. Every new thought, every "caesura" (Bion, 1976, p. 296), including the caesura of birth, every experience of joy, surprise, emotional turbulence, turmoil, or breakdown, is an opportunity to live reality freshly.

Bion, in his late works, views birth as one of the most dramatic caesuras of an individual's life, and like all other caesuras, it is an opportunity to live reality in a way that is fresh, turbulent, exquisitely alive. Birth is inevitably experienced as "excessive" (Bion, 1976, p. 296). It requires some degree of repression, and "repression is a kind of a death" (p. 296). Nevertheless, despite inevitable repression, birth is life opening into something as new as "the invocation of Light at the start of the Third Book [of Milton's *Paradise Lost*], 'Won from the void and formless infinite'" (Bion, 1976, p. 296).

From this perspective, the infant is not simply born unformed and in need of help from the mother to organize, to "contain" (Bion, 1962b, 1970), his experience, as the infant is in "early Bion." I would add, though Bion never puts it this way, the infant is "an innocent," in the best sense of the word. That is, he is not nearly as weighed down with "understanding" as he very shortly will be, and as adults certainly are. Given the infant's *relative* freedom from "understandings," his way of experiencing/becoming is fresh and immediate and lively (if helped by his mother with his "unthinkable thoughts," as described in the work of "early Bion"). But the infant's experience at birth is also turbulent and distressing, which leads the infant, at times, to resort to repression, "a kind of death."

This conception of the emergence of mind, which places emphasis on the need not to know, not to understand, and instead to become the reality of what is occurring, adds a new dimension to the understanding of the emergence of mind found in Bion's early work, but it does not replace the earlier one; rather, it stands in dialectical tension with its more linear (hermeneutic) counterpart.

Concluding comment

The stories of the emergence of mind according to Freud, Klein, Fairbairn, Winnicott, and Bion have embedded in them concepts of mind, which I have articulated. I have traced a movement in the analytic conception of mind from that of an apparatus for thinking and for coping with internal and external pressures (in the work of Freud, Klein, and Fairbairn) to that of a concept of mind as a process, an ongoing experience of being alive to the present moment (in the work of Winnicott and Bion). This evolution in analytic thought is integral to a new and vital stage in the development of psychoanalysis in which an emphasis on epistemological thinking and practice (having to do with knowing and understanding) is shifting toward an emphasis on ontological thinking and practice (having to do with being and becoming).

References

Bion, W. R. (1962a). A theory of thinking. In *Second Thoughts*. New York: Aronson, pp. 110–119.

Bion, W. R. (1962b) *Learning from Experience*. London: Tavistock.

Bion, W. R. (1963). *Elements of Psychoanalysis*. London: Tavistock.

Bion, W. R. (1965). *Transformations: Change from Learning to Growth*. London: Tavistock.

Bion, W. R. (1967). Notes on memory and desire. In *Wilfred Bion: Los Angeles Seminars and Supervision*, edited by Aguayo, J. & Malin, B. London: Karnac, 2013, pp. 136–138.

Bion, W. R. (1970). *Attention and Interpretation*. London: Tavistock.

Bion, W. R. (1976). Emotional turbulence. In *Clinical Seminars and Other Works*, edited by Bion, F. London: Karnac, pp. 293–332.

Fairbairn, W. R. D. (1940). Schizoid factors in the personality. In *Psychoanalytic Studies of the Personality*. London: Routledge and Kegan Paul, 1952, pp. 3–27.

Fairbairn, W. R. D. (1944). Endopsychic structure considered in terms of object-relationships. In *Psychoanalytic Studies of the Personality*. London: Routledge and Kegan Paul, 1952, p. 82–132.

Fairbairn, W. R. D. (1958). On the nature and aims of psychoanalytical treatment. *The International Journal of Psychoanalysis*, 39:374–385.

Fairbairn, W. R. D. (1963). Synopsis of an object–relations theory of the personality. *The International Journal of Psychoanalysis*, 44:224–225.

Freud, S. (1900). The interpretation of dreams. SE, 4–5.

Freud, S. (1905). Three essays on the theory of sexuality. SE, 7.

Freud, S. (1911a). Formulations on the two principles of mental functioning. SE, 12.

Freud, S. (1911b). The history of the psychoanalytical movement. SE, 14

Freud, S. (1915a). Instincts and their vicissitudes. SE, 14.

Freud, S. (1915b). Repression. SE, 14.

Freud, S. (1923). The ego and the id. SE, 12.

Freud, S. (1929). Civilization and its discontents. SE, 21.

Freud, S. (1940). An outline of psychoanalysis. SE 22.

Habermas, J. (1971). *Knowledge and Human Interests*, Shapiro, J. (trans.). Boston, MA: Beacon Press.

Isaacs, S. (1952). The nature and function of phantasy. In *Developments in Psycho-analysis*, edited by Rivière. London: Hogarth Press, 1952, pp. 62–121.

Klein, M. (1934). A contribution to the psychogenesis of manic–depressive states. In *Contributions to Psycho-Analysis, 1921–1945*. London: Hogarth Press, 1958, pp. 282–311.

Klein, M (1946). Notes on some schizoid mechanisms. In *Envy and Gratitude and Other Works, 1946–1963*. New York: Delacorte Press/ Seymour Laurence, 1975, pp. 1–24.

Klein, M. (1952a). The mutual influences in the development of ego and id. In *Envy and Gratitude and Other Works, 1946–1963*. New York: Delacorte Press/Seymour Laurence, 1975, pp. 57–60.

Klein, M. (1952b). Some theoretical conclusions regarding the emotional life of the infant. In *Envy and Gratitude and Other Works, 1946–1963*. New York: Delacorte Press/Seymour Laurence, 1975, pp. 61–93.

Klein, M (1955). On identification. In *Envy and Gratitude and Other Works, 1946–1963*. New York: Delacorte Press/Seymour Laurence, 1975, pp. 141–175.

Klein, M. (1957). Envy and gratitude. In *Envy and Gratitude and Other Works, 1946–1963*. New York: Delacorte Press/Seymour Laurence, 1975, pp. 176–236.

Klein, M. (1958). On the development of mental functioning. In *Envy and Gratitude and Other Works, 1946–1963*. New York: Delacorte Press/ Seymour Laurence, 1975, pp. 236–246.

Klein, M. (1963). On the sense of loneliness. In *Envy and Gratitude and Other Works, 1946–1963*. New York: Delacorte Press/Seymour Laurence, 1975, pp. 300–313.

Laplanche, J. and Pontalis, J.-B. (1973). *The Language of Psycho-Analysis*, Nicholson-Smith, D. (trans.). New York: Norton.

Ogden, T. H. (1992). The dialectically constituted/decentred subject of psychoanalysis. I. The Freudian subject. *The International Journal of Psychoanalysis*, 73: 517–526.

Ogden, T. H. (2010). Why read Fairbairn? *The International Journal of Psychoanalysis*, 91:101–118.

Poe, E. A. (1848). To _____ _____ _____. In *The Complete Tales and Poems of Edgar Allan Poe*. New York, NY: Barnes and Noble, 1992, p. 80.

Ricoeur, P. (1981). *Hermeneutics and the Human Sciences: Essays on Language, Action and Interpretation*. Cambridge, UK: Cambridge University Press.

Segal, H. (1964). *Introduction to the Work of Melanie Klein*. London: Hogarth Press.

Winnicott, D. W. (1947). Hate in the countertransference. In *Through Paediatrics to Psycho-Analysis*. New York: Basic Books, 1965, pp. 194–203.

Winnicott, D. W. (1949). Mind and its relation to the psyche-soma. In *Through Paediatrics to Psycho-Analysis*. New York: Basic Books, 1965, pp. 243–254.

Winnicott, D. W. (1953). Transitional objects and transitional phenomena. In *Playing and Reality*. New York: Basic Books, 1971, pp. 1–25.

Winnicott, D. W. (1956). Primary maternal preoccupation. In *Through Paediatrics to Psycho-Analysis*. New York: Basic Books, 1965, pp. 300–305.

Winnicott, D. W. (1963). Communicating and not communicating leading to a study of certain opposites. In *The Maturational Processes and the Facilitating Environment*. New York: International Universities Press, 1965, pp. 179–192.

Winnicott, D. W. (1964). *The Child, the Family, and the Outside World*. Baltimore, MD: Pelican Books.

Winnicott, D. W. (1971a). Transitional objects and transitional phenomena. In *Playing and Reality*. New York: Basic Books, pp. 1–25.

Winnicott, D. W. (1971b). The place where we live. In *Playing and Reality*. New York: Basic Books, pp. 104–110.

Winnicott, D. W. (1971c). Introduction. In *Playing and Reality*. New York: Basic Books, pp. xi–xiii.

7

ON LANGUAGE AND TRUTH IN PSYCHOANALYSIS

Psychoanalysis as a therapeutic process centers much of its energy on helping the patient experience, and give voice to, a truth that has been disturbing him for much of his life, a truth that he has been unable to think or feel because it has been too much to bear. Language plays a pivotal role in bringing to life the emotional truth of previously unbearable experience in the analytic session.

The patient and analyst develop ways of talking to one another and use those ways of talking to get at the truth as it is lived in the session. I discuss three ways that my patients and I have talked to one another, which I call *direct discourse, tangential discourse*, and *discourse in non sequiturs*.

The language that patient and analyst use in talking with one another is an inherent part of the experience of the truth, and the truth of the experience, of any session. To put it in slightly different words, the ways in which patients and analysts talk to one another, including all that is not said but expressed in tone of voice or in what is left to the imagination, is an integral part of what is happening in the session.

I take as a starting point for this discussion the idea that human beings are fundamentally truth-seeking animals, though we are afraid of the truth in almost but not quite equal measure. I will be discussing particular forms of discourse that enable the patient to experience *with the analyst* the truth that the patient has previously been unable to think or feel, much less put into words, on his own. Often the truth of the session involves events that the patient has not yet been able to experience (Winnicott, 1974) and consequently remain "unlived" (Ogden, 2014) aspects of the patient's life.

DOI: 10.4324/9781003228462-7

There are innumerable forms of discourse (a term I use inter-changeably with *dialogue* and *conversation*). I will be addressing only the three I mentioned: direct discourse, tangential discourse, and discourse in the form of non sequiturs. (I have invented the names for these types of discourse as a form of shorthand with which to discuss the similarities and differences among these ways of con-versing.) All three of these forms derive their shape from the very structure of language, a structure that inherently involves an active interplay of manifest and implicit meaning.

In the analytic setting, the experience of the truth is shaped, colored, textured, structured, and so on, by language. Patient and analyst develop forms of discourse that not only serve as the medium in which the truth is conveyed; the discourse itself is a critical part of the truth of what is occurring at any given moment of a session. Each form of discourse is expressive of a truth that bears its mark. In the present chapter, I am not simply illustrating three different forms of analytic discourse; I am hoping to convey a sense of the ways in which three of my patients and I developed different ways of talking with one another that were unique to the work I did with each of them, and allowed us to bring to life the truth of what was occur-ring between us.

While each of the three forms of discourse that I will discuss serves to express the truth in its own distinctive way, all three, to my mind, hold in common the following quality: the medium for the communication of the truth is not to be found primarily in the declaratives, in the story being told, but in the parts left out, in the breaks in the discourse. What I have in mind when I refer to the breaks in the discourse are the places where there is disjunction—sometimes a lack of correspondence between the words and their usual meanings, at other times a seemingly incomprehensible gap between what one person says and how the other responds, and at still other times a divide between the feeling or idea that is expected and the one that is actually stated or implied.

When these and other sorts of disjunctions occur in the discourse between patient and analyst, an emotional climate is generated in which both participants experience some degree of feeling lost, confused, perplexed, at sea, and almost always mystified. Mystified because patient and analyst, at points of break in expected coher-ence of dialogue, not only feel shaken, they also experience a feeling of marvel in the face of the unknown, in the face of unanticipated possibilities. The analytic pair can no longer rely on what they thought they knew, for what they have known no longer feels sufficient to meaningfully contain the elements of experience now in play. They must either attempt to deaden, obscure, and ignore what is occurring in the break, or attempt to make themselves open and vulnerable to something of the reality, the truth, of what is happening.

The truth sensed in the breaks is merely suggested, as if perceived through a mist in which discernible shapes are vague, but doubtlessly real, doubtlessly true. The imperfectly perceived truth leaves the individual feeling a combination of amazement and fear. The truth of the individual's experience that is nascent in the moment cannot be passively "taken in" in a moment of epiphany; unconscious psychological work must be done. What is true to that moment must be created psychically—"dreamt up"—as patient and analyst together engage in the conscious and unconscious experience of being changed by the truth of the moment, a truth that is always on the move, accruing verbally symbolic meanings as it goes.

The analytic setting—with its unstructured mode of conversation; the maximization of the role of language and sound by means of the patient's use of the couch; the effort to release analyst and patient from the hegemony of secondary process thinking, and in so doing, allowing waking dreaming (reverie) to become a form of intrasubjective and intersubjective communication—all of this together is designed to help the analytic pair enter into a state of mind in which an experience of the truth, and the truth of the experience, may unfold, both in the form of what is said and what is left out.

Before proceeding to a detailed discussion of different forms of discourse, I would like to offer three clarifications. First, when I speak of patient and analyst "dreaming" together, I am referring to their unconsciously thinking and feeling, individually and collectively, the truth of an experience that was, for the patient, previously unthinkable. To my mind, this overlap of the dreaming of patient and analyst lies at the heart of the analytic experience (see Ogden, 1997, 2004, 2007, for discussions and illustrations of patient and analyst "dreaming up" the truth of an experience together).

Second, the unconscious, in the way I understand the term, is an aspect of mind capable of realistically perceiving internal and external reality, and encompassing the two in the process of generating a form of psychic reality that I think of as the psychic truth of one's experience.

Third, it is essential not to overvalue the names I have given to the three forms of discourse that I will discuss. I am not wedded to the terminology, nor do I see clear dividing lines that indicate precisely when a segment of dialogue ceases to be direct discourse and becomes tangential discourse, and when tangential discourse begins to be discourse of non sequiturs.

Direct discourse

The manifest level of a conversation consisting of a series of direct responses *appears* to limit itself strictly to questions and statements pertaining to the subject at hand.

I think of this exchange as *direct discourse* because of its form—a series of declarative sentences and questions with little in the way of metaphor, visual imagery, irony, wit, syntactical variety, and so on. And yet direct discourse may succeed in conveying a truth that can only be created in this form of exchange.

I will now turn to an analytic experience in which direct discourse played a prominent role in creating an experience of the truth, which evolved in the course of the analysis.

In the early stages of analytic work, Ms. V described the neglect and verbal abuse that she had received at the hands of her mother, and the isolation she experienced in response to the absence of her father, who was home only briefly between lecture tours. Once she had given me all the "history" that she could "recall," she felt at a loss regarding "what more to say." She then adopted a pattern of describing in detail the events that had occurred in the interval between her sessions.

After more than a year of this five-sessions-per-week analysis, I was reminded, as Ms. V was talking, of a comment made by a beloved, deceased mentor of mine who had said that when this sort of description of daily life went on too long, he felt tempted to say, "And how much salt, Mrs. Jones, did you say you put on your green beans?" I was struck for the first time, as the remark came to me during this session with Ms. V, that it was addressed to "Mrs. Jones," an imaginary patient—it was a joke, after all—but the fact that it was not addressed to a real patient caught my attention.

The deprecating nature of my mentor's comment also struck me in a way that was different from the ways it had before, in that it resonated with my already growing feeling that Ms. V's listing of her activities was meant to provoke anger in me. It seemed to me that the patient was unable to experience feelings of her own, and was trying to evoke them in me in her stead—most prominently, feelings of anger and despair. The importance of my recalling my mentor's comment at that particular juncture, in conjunction with intense feelings of missing him, led me to bring into focus for myself how lonely I felt while sitting with Ms. V.

As these thoughts and feelings came to me during the course of the second year of analysis, I found myself talking to Ms. V in a way that was unusual for me. I repeatedly asked her to tell me what she was feeling during one of the seemingly endless series of events she was describing—for example, by inquiring, "How did you feel when J [a man she had been dating for six months] was yelling at you?"

The patient would give me one-word replies to my questions, such as "angry," "scared," "disappointed," "horrified." I said to Ms. V in exasperation at one point, "Your naming a feeling, and then saying nothing further about it, feels as if you're trying to provoke anger in me, which would result in my feeling something that would substitute for your having a feeling of your own."

Ms. V said, without pause, "That's right. I do that a lot." This response seemed to me at the time to be a continuation of the patient's provocations. I recognized that, in my persistent questioning of Ms. V, I was trying to get blood from a stone, just as she had attempted in vain to extract love from her mother and father. Even though my comment was in some ways accurate, it failed to capture the truth of the moment because it was spoken in a way that was belittling of the patient.

One day during this period of analysis, in response to the patient's telling me she felt "sad" when a friend said she was unable to attend an event with her, I asked, "Did you really feel sad?"

Ms. V was silent for some time, which was unusual for her. She then said, "When you ask me how I'm feeling, I say what I think a person should feel, or what I think *you* think I should be feeling, but I really don't feel anything." I said, "What you're saying to me now seems to me to be one of the first truthful things you've ever said to me." The patient said, "Yes, it feels that way to me, too." I asked, "Do you really believe that?" She said, "I don't know." The sound of the patient's voice, as she spoke those words, felt sadly true to me.

In this period of work with Ms. V, there was a predominance of direct discourse ("What are you feeling?" "Anxious."). There were many ways in which the patient and I were protecting ourselves from the truth of the emptiness and despair of the situation we were in. She tried to elicit from me, sometimes successfully, anger-filled statements that helped her experience my statements as expressions of emotions she felt incapable of feeling and felt she should be feeling. For my part, I engaged in imaginary conversation with my mentor with whom I had had a real exchange of thoughts and feelings, though it was significant that this "conversation" was with a person who was dead.

Once Ms. V and I became better able to talk with one another about her feeling that she was unable to feel emotion, our conversations felt more real and alive. She said, at one point, "My father was a somebody, I'm a nobody." Ms. V had not been aware, until the words came out of her mouth, of the double meaning of the word "nobody" in her sentence. This was one of many instances in which Ms. V's way of talking became more interesting in this period of analytic work. Words carried layers of meaning, when earlier they had felt as if they carried only literal meaning or less than literal meaning (empty verbiage). Direct discourse began to be infused with life as it was spoken with feeling that rang true ("I don't know [if I believe what I said]"), and gestured toward a truth not yet known (what is it *for her* to be nobody?). The form of our discourse—simple declarative sentences in which there was only sparse imagery, metaphor, wit, and the like—did not change very much at this juncture in the analysis. What changed was the way we spoke these rather unadorned sentences, and the range of feelings and ideas communicated and elicited by them.

Tangential discourse

When two people are engaged in what I am calling *tangential discourse*, responses on the part of both participants glance off "the subject" (in both senses of the word) and allude to other subjects, other meanings, other people. Metaphor, simile, irony, wit, ambiguity, hyperbole, unexpected word choice, syntactical shifts, errors in grammar or verb tense—all these events in language and many more make up the sorts of language usage found in the realm of *tangential discourse*. This type of discourse lives in the realm of metaphor, the realm of one feeling or idea or image becoming linked with (transferred to) another, and in so doing, creating new meaning in the space that is created between the two elements being linked to one another.

The word *metaphor* is derived from the Greek *meta* (across or beyond) and *pherein* (to bear or transfer). In tangential discourse, we carry meanings across or beyond the border of the apparent subject of conversation to another subject. Sometimes, in literature, a neologism performs this metaphorical work. For instance, Shakespeare, in *The Tempest* (1610), invented the word *sea-change* (1.2.400), for which I believe there is no translation. *The New Shorter Oxford English Dictionary* (1993) tells us that sea-change means "radical change" (p. 2742), but the word *sea-change* and the phrase *radical change* are not at all the same. It is impossible to find other words to express the meaning of sea-change, a word that alludes to the sea, but the sea is so many things: it is vast and powerful, it ebbs exactly as much as it flows, it kills and gives life, and so forth. Metaphor creates a space between the two things being compared, and in that space meanings proliferate.

So, too, in the case of dreams, we cannot say what a dream "really" means. Dreams are what they are. Like the metaphor embedded in the word *sea-change*, dreams allude to meaning, but refuse to be reduced to a meaning or even a set of meanings. This is what is difficult and wondrous about dreams and reveries. They allude to unconscious meaning, but they never define it, spell it out, or serve as translations or decodings of it. They are predominantly a visual experience for which no words suffice as an expression of that experience. Dreams and reveries are metaphors for unconscious thoughts and feelings. We are dreaming all the time, both when we are awake and asleep (Bion, 1962), and consequently, we are all the time engaged in metaphor-making.

In the act of dreaming, we carry meaning "beyond" the limits of one order of experiencing (the visual experience of dreaming the dream) to another (the largely verbal experience of "understanding" the dream [Grotstein, 2000; Sandler, 1976]). But I believe that the term *understanding* is a misnomer for what we do with our dreaming experience. We never *know* or *understand* unconscious experience because unconscious experience is, by definition, inaccessible to consciousness. I believe it is more accurate to say that we are some-times able to *experience metaphoric renderings of* the unconscious, which spew meaning (often surprising and disturbing meaning) forward and backward in time. As is the case with a poem, there are no other words with which to say it, explain it, understand it, translate it, paraphrase it, or the like. A poem is immutably itself, as is a dream.

Turning now to tangential discourse in the analytic setting, I will present a fragment of an analysis that occurred at a time in which the patient, Mr. Q, and I had come to know one another quite well over the course of many years of analysis. He was a reclusive man who, when he began analysis, seemed to have relationships exclu-sively with figures in his internal world; his relationship with me had consisted almost entirely of projections of those figures onto me and into me, which often led me to feel taken over by them in an oppressive way. He had told me in the beginning that, ideally, he would have an analysis in the form of slipping under my door a piece of paper on which he had written something he wanted to say, and after reading it, I would slip a piece of paper back under the door to him with my response written on it.

Several years into this analysis, I met Mr. Q in the waiting room and said, "Hi" to him, as I always did. When I said, "Hi" (not "Hello") to Mr. Q one morning, I was oddly aware that in saying "Hi" in the way I did, I was as usual trying to inject life into my voice, but was feeling the flatness of my attempt and was anticipating that I would get nothing in return from Mr. Q. I was aware on that particular day that I did not use the patient's name as I greeted him. I rarely address patients by their name—first name or surname—so it was a mystery to me why I would notice that absence with Mr. Q on that particular day.

All of this occurred as I said the word "Hi" and as Mr. Q silently rose from his chair without looking at me. As I looked at him, his rising from his chair seemed almost begrudging, and yet I could feel that I liked him, even as I was feeling locked out by him.

In his usual way, he made no verbal response to my greeting, nor did he lift his gaze from the floor as he stood and led the way into my consulting room. Halfway to the couch, he mumbled, with his back to me, "How are you?"

It struck me, as he said these words, that in using the personal pronoun "you," he was, in a sense, speaking my name for the first time. I could not remember his ever using that pronoun in that way, much less asking me how I was. I did not know what I was going to say until I heard the words come from my mouth.

I began by saying, "I'm good." But on hearing those words, I felt a need to tell the patient that I recognized all that was entailed in his response to me, so I said (again without formulating it ahead of time), "I'm very good." I thought, after I said these words, that it would have been condescending to congratulate Mr. Q for saying, "How are you?" but in saying, "I'm very good," I was telling him (in a somewhat disguised way) that I recognized the risk he had taken in expressing his recognition of me and the beginnings of his feeling concern for me.

I think of my "two-part response" to Mr. Q's question as a direct response followed by a tangential one. The second part of the response, "I'm very good," glanced off the "subjects" of his question (me and my well-being) to say something about new "subjects" (Mr. Q and his question).

My questions to myself, as I said "Hi" to Mr. Q in the waiting room, reflected the ways in which I was unconsciously in a state of flux in my ability to face the truth of the ways I had closed myself off to Mr. Q, perhaps out of fear of feeling humiliated by his turning his back on my feelings of affection for him. I had "known" that Mr. Q had experienced the humiliation of having his love ignored and rejected by his mother, and that part of him had died as a result, but I had never *really known* his fear of being humiliated in this way until I felt subjected to a version of it myself.

My saying "I'm very good" offered a response to the unconscious meanings of his statement (in the form of a question), which had to do with his hope that I would feel the truth of the highly personal event that was occurring, and would give him an equally personal and truthful response. My two-part response, "I'm good" and then "I'm very good," opened a space of its own (though not as striking and surprising a space as Mr. Q's question/statement had opened). In the second part of my response, I reached for something more personal, something that felt as if it were made specifically for Mr. Q under these circumstances. The space my two-part response opened was unique to Mr. Q and me, and to our joint effort to say more of the truth than we had ever said before, without saying too much too soon. It was an open invitation (and an invitation to open ourselves) to reach for more in our efforts to speak to one another the truth of our feelings for each other.

In the years that followed that exchange, Mr. Q told me several times how important that session was to him. He said that he had said "the question" to himself many times before he was able to say it to me. (His use of the words "the question" made me think of a wedding proposal, "popping the question.") Only at that point did I recognize that Mr. Q's question was not the literal "How are you?" but rather the metaphorical "Who are you?" I wished I could have sensed that, and found a way of responding to it, years earlier when he asked me how I was.

In a session much later in our work, he said, "I didn't know you then. I didn't know what to expect. If you had just given me an impersonal or canned response, I don't know that I could have ever come back." In the silence that followed his saying this, I felt an intense feeling of sorrow. I could feel, and I think he could, too, that he was, without spelling it out, referring to his sense that he had died in childhood and would never completely "come back" from that.

In subsequent years, in this long analysis, Mr. Q developed, or slowly showed me—I never could be sure which it was—a wry sense of humor. We laughed deeply together. On one occasion, I could not stop myself from laughing at several points later in the session when the mood of that earlier laughter returned to me. We both could feel at these times that he was feeling real and alive, feelings that until recently he had never experienced.

Discourse of non sequiturs

In the analytic setting, discourse in the form of non sequiturs is an extreme form of tangential discourse in which the connection between the two thoughts or feelings making up the (seeming) non sequitur pushes the envelope of comprehensibility; and yet the non sequitur manages to open a space in which previously unexpressed thoughts and feelings may be communicated. I use the word *seeming* to modify the term *non sequitur* because the gap between the two statements that form the non sequitur is unintelligible from the point of view of the conscious mind, but to some extent intelligible from the point of view of the unconscious mind. I will not always use the word *seeming* to modify *non sequitur*, but the modifier is always implied.

The fact that the truth communicated in the form of a non sequitur is unconsciously grasped by patient and analyst, at least to some degree, does not mean that the psychic truth communicated in this way is not disturbing to both of them. Quite the contrary— unrecognized truths are unrecognized because they have been too painful to bear.

Communication by means of non sequitur is a form of discourse in which meaning is obliquely suggested. It requires that the two people engaged in this form of discourse (which never occurs in pure form) do a good deal of unconscious psychological work as they are encompassing, as a pair, the seemingly disconnected elements of the non sequitur. Such conversation has a deeply intimate quality. Only the two people engaged in this kind of discourse are able to experience the full range and depth of feeling encompassed by the way they are using language. An imaginary eavesdropper on this form of conversation hears primarily the conscious level of the communication (which makes "little sense") because patient and analyst are together generating and thinking about unconscious meanings that only they are privy to.

While non sequiturs both create and traverse a divide, that divide need not announce itself in an obvious way; it may go unnoticed *consciously* by the two people conversing, but it never goes unnoticed by them *unconsciously*.

What follows is a segment of dialogue in which discourse by non sequitur is the dominant, but by no means the only, form of discourse taking place. I have excerpted a portion of a much longer exchange that I have previously discussed in connection with the idea of working without memory or desire (Ogden, 2015). Here I will put in square brackets my thoughts concerning the nature of the discourse taking place in this portion of the session.

I had been working with Ms. C for several years in a five-sessions-per-week analysis when this exchange occurred. About a year before the analysis began, Ms. C, who had no other children, had had a miscarriage four and a half months into her pregnancy, which had left her severely depressed. She felt that her body was telling her that she was unfit to be a mother. In the course of our work, Ms. C's depression lifted significantly, but she still held steadfastly to the belief that she was unfit to be a mother. She doubted her capacity to love or to be worthy of anyone else's love, particularly the love of her dead baby.

On meeting Ms. C in the waiting room, I had the feeling that she was in the wrong place, and that I should tell her politely that the person she had come to see was located in another building on the same block as mine. This feeling was particularly puzzling because I was fond of Ms. C, and I almost always looked forward to seeing her for her sessions.

When the patient lay down on the couch that day, I had the impulse to say, "I love you." [These thoughts and feelings may seem odd to the reader, as they did to me, but they also felt natural to me at the time. There was not time to try to grasp in the moment what it meant that I was feeling that the patient was in the wrong place and should be seeing a therapist down the block, or to try to understand why I felt the impulse to tell her I loved her. I felt that I was in the grip of something I did not understand, but at the same time, I felt open to allowing these thoughts and feelings to take what course they would.]

In response to Ms. C's telling me a dream in which she had lost something, but did not know what she had lost, I said, "Is loving me such a terrible thing that you have to leave it somewhere else when you come to see me?" [I had not planned to say this to the patient, but it felt true as I said it. Ms. C and I were now talking with one another in a discourse of (seeming) non sequiturs in which unconscious truth linked what was left out of the manifest level of what we were saying to one another.]

Without pause, Ms. C responded by saying, "You've never told me that you love me before." [Of course, I had not told her I loved her, but I had in fact imagined saying it to her. What I had actually told her in the sentence just cited was that I thought she felt that "loving me" was a "terrible thing" for her to bring into the room with me, so she left it somewhere else before coming to see me. This comment was a spontaneous (non sequitur) response to the patient's dream in which she lost something, but did not know what it was. My comment was also informed by the feeling I had had in the waiting room that Ms. C (her love) was in the wrong place, and should be "down the street" with someone else.]

I said, "Would my love be in the wrong place if I were to love you?" [This non sequitur was my way of saying to Ms. C (in the form of a semi–rhetorical question) that, despite her feelings to the contrary, it might be that she was worthy of my love, which in this moment was inseparable from being worthy of the love of her dead baby.]

The patient said, "Yes, I think it would, but I would feel empty if I were to give it back." [Here the patient was saying that my love (and her dead baby's love) would be misplaced if it were directed at her. But she was saying more than that. She was adding something very complex and ambiguous. Ms. C was saying that she would feel empty if she could not accept my love (that is, if she were to "give it back" to me unreciprocated); *and* she would feel empty if she were able to reciprocate ("give back") my love. Why she would feel empty if she were to reciprocate my love and her baby's love was still a mystery.]

Because my commentary disrupts the flow of (seeming) non sequiturs, I will provide the uninterrupted dialogue in order to re-create something closer to my experience in the session:

> In response to Ms. C's telling me a dream in which she had lost something, but didn't know what she had lost, I said, "Is loving me such a terrible thing that you have to leave it somewhere else when you come to see me?"
>
> Without pause, Ms. C responded by saying, "You've never told me that you love me before."
>
> I said, "Would my love be in the wrong place if I were to love you?"
>
> Ms. C said, "Yes, I think it would, but I would feel empty if I were to give it back."

Without the unconscious linkages underlying this series of non sequiturs, the exchange is baffling. But even when I add to the sentences that the patient and I actually spoke—add my own unspoken thoughts and feelings, and my very tentative grasp of what was happening at an unconscious level in this dialogue—there remains much that is "unexplained." This is so because unconscious thoughts and feelings are "inexplicable"—untranslatable into conscious, secondary process narratives. Discourse in the form of non sequitur, I believe, closely reflects unconscious experience because, in a discourse of non sequiturs, there are far fewer linkages between lived experience and verbally symbolic meaning than in direct discourse, or even in tangential discourse. So much more is left to the imagination in this form of discourse. The "commentary" I have offered in my discussion of the very brief exchange between Ms. C and me reads like a poor translation of an ancient language no longer spoken, but which is nonetheless the foundation of the language we are currently speaking.

Concluding comments

The way in which patient and analyst talk to one another (the form of discourse in which they engage) is not simply a way of conveying the truth of what is happening at a given moment in the session. The experience of talking together in a particular way (the experience of a particular form of discourse) is itself an integral part of the truth of what is occurring at that moment in the session. I have discussed three forms of discourse in the analytic setting—direct discourse, tangential discourse, and discourse in the form of non sequitur. Each of these forms of discourse involves a different form of closeness between patient and analyst, none necessarily involving greater intimacy than the others, but each involving a different type of intimacy.

The truth in the analytic setting is extremely difficult and painful to experience and express, for the truth that the patient seeks when asking an analyst for help is the truth of experiences that were unbearable when they occurred, and remain unbearable. Every analytic pair is engaged from the outset in the task of creating a way of talking together that is adequate to give expression both to the patient's fear of the truth and to the patient's need to know the truth of his or her experience.

References

Bion, W. R. (1962). *Learning from Experience*. London: Tavistock.

Grotstein, J. S. (2000). *Who Is the Dreamer Who Dreams the Dream? A Study of Psychic Presences*. Hillsdale, NJ: Analytic Press.

The New Shorter Oxford English Dictionary (1993). Oxford, UK: Clarendon Press.

Ogden, T. H. (1997). Reverie and interpretation. *The Psychoanalytic Quarterly*, 66:567–595.

Ogden, T. H. (2004). This art of psychoanalysis: Dreaming undreamt dreams and interrupted cries. *The International Journal of Psychoanalysis*, 85:857–878.

Ogden, T. H. (2007). On talking-as-dreaming. *The International Journal of Psychoanalysis*, 88:575–589.

Ogden, T. H. (2014). Fear of breakdown and the unlived life. *The International Journal of Psychoanalysis*, 95:205–224.

Ogden, T. H. (2015). Intuiting the truth of what's happening: On Bion's "Notes on Memory and Desire." *The Psychoanalytic Quarterly*, 84:285–306.

Sandler, J. (1976). Dreams, unconscious fantasies and "identity of perception." *The International Review of Psycho-Analysis*, 3:33–42.

Shakespeare, W. (1610). *The Tempest*. In *The Comedies of William Shakespeare*. New York: Modern Library, 1994.

Winnicott, D. W. (1974). Fear of breakdown. *The International Review of Psycho-Analysis*, 1:103–107.

8

EXPERIENCING THE POETRY OF ROBERT FROST AND EMILY DICKINSON

In this brief chapter I will be putting aside questions concerning how reading poetry informs the way one listens to patients and oneself while practicing psychoanalysis, and how the practice of psychoanalysis informs the way one reads poetry. My interest, here, is in the way a poem affects the reader, and how the poem creates those effects. In the discussions of poems by Robert Frost and Emily Dickinson that follow, I hope that the reader will experience some of the sheer pleasure and wonder that I find in these poems (a good deal of which lies in the visage of death).

A poem by Robert Frost

The first of the poems I will discuss, Robert Frost's (1923) "Stopping by woods on a snowy evening," may seem like a surprising choice of poem. It is a poem that school children used to memorize and recite. This and other "well-known" poems by Frost contributed to his having been, for a long time, viewed by the literary establishment as a minor poet who "has written *good* poems that ordinary readers like without any trouble and understand without any trouble" (Jarrell, 1953, p. 26). Randall Jarrell was the first major literary critic to discover "the other Frost" (p. 26), the Frost whose best

> poetry *is* like the world, "the world wherein we find our happiness or not at all," the world with its animals and plants and, most of all its people: people working, thinking about things,

 DOI: 10.4324/9781003228462-8

falling in love, taking naps; in these poems people are not only the glory and jest and riddle of the world, but also the habit of the world, its strange ordinariness, its ordinary strangeness, and they too trudge down the ruts along which the planets move in their courses.

(Jarrell, 1953, p. 61)

Stopping by woods on a snowy evening

Whose woods these are I think I know.
His house is in the village though;
He will not see me stopping here
To watch his woods fill up with snow.

My little horse must think it queer
To stop without a farmhouse near
Between the woods and frozen lake
The darkest evening of the year.

He gives his harness bell a shake
To ask if there is some mistake.
The only other sound's the sweep
Of easy wind and downy flake.

The woods are lovely, dark and deep.
But I have promises to keep,
And miles to go before I sleep,
And miles to go before I sleep.

The first line of the poem—"Whose woods these are I think I know"—is a full sentence, which gives the line authority. But that authority is at the same time undercut by the final words of the line: "I think I know." (The use of the present tense gives immediacy and quiet intensity to the poem—we are there with the speaker in the woods at night.) The effect of the second line—"His house is in the village though"—is the beginning of a series of subtle descents into the experience of being alone in vast darkness, this time in the form of the absence of the owner (whose house is in town). By the time we reach the final line of the second stanza, the softness of the words

157

"Snowy evening" (in the title of the poem) is supplanted by something far more ominous: "The darkest evening of the year."

In the third stanza, what begins as a sense that there is something wrong—"He gives his harness bell a shake"—becomes a terrifying question: "To ask if there is some mistake." That question, for me, conjures up an image of being told I have a terminal illness, and my plaintively asking if this diagnosis could be just "some [terrible] mistake."

The final lines of the third stanza—"The only other sound's the sweep/ Of easy wind and downy flake"—are the beginning of a set of lulling sounds and images that have the effect of drawing the speaker and reader into the darkness and the "frozen lake." The heavy iambic tetrameter of each line—da dum, da dum, da dum, da dum—and the hard rhyming of the last words of the first, second, and fourth lines of each of the first three stanzas, combine to create a feeling of a forced march toward the unstoppable, the inevitable.

The fourth stanza mirrors the first in that its opening line holds the authority of a complete sentence: "The woods are lovely, dark and deep." The mesmerizing ("lovely") lure of the unknowable ("dark"), the all-consuming ("deep") woods are now complete. And yet, the sentence that follows begins with the protest of "But": "But I have promises to keep." The speaker will not go willingly—there is too much to be done before he submits to death. A sense of the futility of the protest and the absolute power of the pull of the dark woods is achieved in an astoundingly simple, absolutely final way: the repetition of "And miles to go before I sleep." (This is the only poem Frost wrote that ends with a repetition of the final line.) The power of this repetition to create a sense of absolute finality is reinforced by the fact that all four lines of the last stanza end with hard rhymes that create the feeling of a final proclamation: "deep," "keep," "sleep," "sleep."

The repeated word "sleep" that ends the poem turns objection into verdict, protest into epitaph, temporality into timelessness.

A poem by Emily Dickinson

Emily Dickinson's poems demand that the reader allow himself or herself to be inhabited by the world created in the poem. I am almost always intrigued, sometimes thrilled, by the opening lines of her poems (all of which are untitled, so the first line hits me particularly hard, coming as if out of nowhere). In the lines that follow that initial line, I regularly find myself in a place I do not quite recognize, or perhaps more accurately, I find an unrecognizable place in myself.

Dickinson's "There's a certain Slant of light," a poem written circa 1861, and first published in 1890, has haunted me and unsettled me for decades. It opens with an astonishing line that is followed by lines that deepen its complex and enigmatic qualities:

> There's a certain Slant of light,
> Winter afternoons—
> That oppresses, like the Heft
> Of Cathedral Tunes—
>
> Heavenly Hurt, it gives us—
> We can find no scar,
> But internal difference,
> Where the Meanings, are—
>
> None may teach it—Any—
> 'Tis the Seal Despair—
> An imperial affliction
> Sent us of the air—
>
> When it comes, the Landscape listens—
> Shadows — hold their breath;
> When it goes, 'tis like the Distance
> On the look of Death—

Everyone has noticed the slanted light of the sun on winter afternoons, but who but Dickinson puts it in her own way, "There's a certain Slant of light," with its spare, conversational ("There's" instead of "There is") simplicity and its musicality (its thrice repeated soft "s" sounds and its loosely iambic meter). The visual image of this particular Slant of light—the only visual image in the poem—is left almost entirely to our imagination, given the fact that the only adjective Dickinson uses is the word "certain." And that adjective modifies the word *Slant* (crowned with a capital "S"), not, as one would expect, the word *light* (with its lowercase "l"). How different the line would be if it read: "There's a certain Slanted light" or "There's a certain Slanting light." In both instances, the meter would be unchanged, but the noun *Slant* would become an adjective (slanted or slanting). *Slant* is far more interesting and unexpected as a noun. Already we are being inhabited by a world different from our own, a world in which light, though still resplendent, has handed over some of its power to its downward gaze. (Dickinson uses no periods in this poem, substituting a double dash [em dash] where one would expect a period or no punctuation at all, which gives the poem an open, airy, yet disjointed quality.)

The mystery of the downward Slant combined with a sense of awe in response to the celestial beauty of the music of the opening line is darkened as we are told that the light "oppresses" "like the Heft/ Of Cathedral Tunes." One can almost hear that "Heft/ Of Cathedral Tunes" (all four words weighed down by their capital letters)—the lumbering pace of a congregation making its way through stolid hymns, dragged along by organ music (downgraded to "Tunes"). Religion offers little comfort in the face of the experience of the downward Slant of light.

In the second stanza, the two sets of feelings—the beauty and the oppressiveness of the Slant of light—are bound to one another in the phrase "Heavenly Hurt." That Hurt leaves no visible scar, but what it does leave is "internal difference/ Where the Meanings, are." "Internal difference"—what an extraordinary way of conveying, without naming it, a sense of the way in which profound emotional pain (perhaps associated with death) leaves its enduring mark in the form of changed relationships among our internal states, and those changed relationships (internal differences) are "Where the Meanings, are." This time the capital letters feel respectful, deferential, but at the same time ironic—do meanings really matter in the end?

This is an unforgiving poem, which after its opening line denies the reader the pleasure of "word music." The poem seems intent on withholding such pleasure. It is a very difficult poem to read aloud because of the unexpected pauses—for instance, the comma after "Meanings" in the line "Where the Meanings, are" and the em dashes before and after "Any" in the first line of the third stanza: "None may teach it—Any—". The latter denies us the flow of the cadence of the words, "None may teach us anything," but in dropping the expected last beat, the word *Any* stands by itself, and is thereby given stern authority.

The line, "Tis the Seal Despair—", in the third stanza, for the first time names a quality of the pain that is experienced in seeing that certain Winter afternoon Slant of light, but enigmatically names it "an imperial affliction," which suggests that this particular pain of despair has not only a personal quality, but also a quality that derives from something "imperial," of a magnitude and power far greater than the merely personal.

The first three lines of the final stanza are suspended between "When it comes" and "When it goes." When the Winter afternoon Slant of light arrives, the inanimate world responds—"the Landscape listens/ Shadows—hold their breath—" (again em dashes prevent us from reading in a lilting fashion, and instead makes us pause, and look, and listen as "the Landscape listens").

The poet could not have chosen a less imagistic word than *Landscape*—the poem grants us not even a leafless tree, a barren hill, or a weathered barn; *Shadows*—not animals, or the wind or the sea—hold their breath. The feeling that the speaker is describing makes the world stand still. But the surprise is in the final two lines, an experience in reading for which the poem, from the outset, has been preparing itself and the reader. The greater difficulty with experiencing despair is not in its coming, but in its going: "When it goes, 'tis like the Distance/ On the look of Death—". We must allow ourselves to be carried by the sound and feel of the words, as opposed to trying to figure out what they mean. What is occurring in the experience of reading is the power generated not by super-imposing images (there is only one image—the downward Slant of light), but by superimposing words and phrases: the "Distance"—a word seized from its ordinary usage and made anew as a particular facial expression (where one might expect a word like *glower* or *glare*)—literally and figuratively lies above "the look of Death" to create what, for me, are the most haunting words in the poem: "the Distance/ On the look of Death—".

The word *Distance* has become more frightening than any imagistic or descriptive word could be at this juncture. It creates for Despair a visage ("the Distance / On the look of Death—") that is unimaginable, impenetrable, indescribable, and yet very real and palpable in the sound of the words, in the way the repetition of the (capitalized) "D" sounds and the sights of the words *Distance* and *Death* create a pounding sound that haunts.

Also, the final word *Death* (what the experience of Despair leaves us with) rhymes with "breath" (the final word of the second line of the stanza). When "it" comes, the Landscape listens; when it goes, the speaker and we readers are left on the very edge of becoming nothing as the sound of the spoken word *Death* disappears into nothingness, just as the poem does not end with a period, but with an em dash. Paradoxically, we cling to our Despair: it is the only alternative to the impending nothingness we feel in that "certain Slant of light,/ Winter afternoons—".

In order to read this poem, I must open myself, unreservedly, to becoming its fierceness, its ferocity, its haunting world in which *I* hold tightly to Despair, even as it is slipping from my grasp, out of fear of the alternative: the nothingness, "the Distance/ On the look of Death—".

★ ★ ★

In reading Frost's and Dickinson's poems, we experience their refusal to please; their combination of subtlety and crushing power: Frost's poem an experience of the futility of protest in the face of death; Dickinson's poem an experience of the futility of the impulse to cling to Despair in the face of the sheer, impersonal inevitability of death.

References

Dickinson, E. (1890). There's a certain Slant of light. In *The Complete Poems of Emily Dickinson*, edited by Johnson, T. H. New York: Back Bay Books/Little Brown, 1960, pp. 118–119.

Frost, R. (1923). Stopping by woods on a snowy evening. In *Robert Frost: Collected Poems, Prose and Plays*, edited by Poirier, R. and Richardson, M. New York: Library of America, 1995, p. 207.

Jarrell, R. (1953). To the Laodiceans. In *Poetry and the Age*. New York: Vintage, 1955, pp. 34–62.

9

ANALYTIC WRITING AS A FORM OF FICTION

Writing, like dreaming, is a medium in which I think and talk to myself in ways I cannot do in any other form. Also, like dreaming, it keeps me alive in my work as a psychoanalyst, for I find that I have to be creating something of my own as I am immersed in trying to help someone else create something of his or her own.

Writing an analytic essay is a very difficult thing to do and requires a great deal of time and effort and anguish. Part of the difficulty is that writing of any sort is autobiographical—after all, where do our feelings, thoughts, and responses originate other than in ourselves? Consequently, analytic writers must put their private world on the page. The better the analytic paper, the more this is the case. I am referring not to information about one's life, but to the life of the writing. An analytic writer, in the very act of writing, is not simply creating a work of art in a particular literary genre; he or she is engaged in a process of being and becoming more fully him- or herself.

Opening oneself up in the act of writing is not enough. One must do something original with one's writing. We must find a way of looking at a situation in our own way, a way that bears our own mark. This is where engagement with language comes in: one creates one's "own mark" solely through the use of language. But the problem facing writers of all sorts is that experience does not present itself in words. Nor do ideas present themselves in organized sentences and paragraphs, much less in the form of an article with an internal structure. One must create something new in order to convey experiences and develop ideas in words and sentences and paragraphs.

DOI: 10.4324/9781003228462-9

In attempting to convey in words something of my own experience while working with a patient, I find that there is nothing more powerful than direct quotation. Since analytic writers do not record sessions (and I do not take notes during sessions), the analytic writer must become a writer of a sort of fiction. The patient presented in an analytic paper (or in a supervisory session or in a consultation group) is not the person lying on the analyst's couch, but an imaginary patient, a fiction, invented in the medium of words, just as a portrait painter creates a work of art, a fiction, an entity in its own right, separate from the person posing for the portrait. To put this in still other words, the written clinical illustration is not the experience with the patient in the analyst's office; it is *like* that experience, a metaphor for it, a fiction.

The analytic writer must invent sentences and verbal exchanges that are *derived from*, but are not transcriptions of, his or her work with a patient (there are few reading experiences more lifeless, for me, than reading the transcript of a recorded analytic session). Analytic writers must invent almost all of the dialogue we write, so in this sense, as I've said, we are writers of fiction. When I use the term *fiction*, I am not referring to falsifying our analytic work; rather, I use the term to refer to writing that attempts to convey what is real and alive, or unreal and dead, about the experience of being with the patient at a given moment in an analysis. In this sense, the fiction that an analytic writer writes is *more true* to the analytic experience than a transcript of the session.

In writing about my experience with patients, I rely on description rather than explanation. Explaining what is occurring in an analytic session tends to lean heavily on cause-and-effect thinking and, consequently, oversimplification; while description, I find, better conveys the nonlinearity and immense complexity of the lived experience with a patient.

Explanations can also lead us to forget that our models of the mind are mere metaphors. There is no such thing as an ego or a superego—these are only ideas, fictions. There is no such thing as a beta-element. There isn't even an internal world—inside what? Inside our head? Between our ears? We are continually making up stories about "the mental apparatus"—and, too often, we believe our stories. We forget that we are creating metaphors, writing fiction. But the fictions we invent—when we are aware they are fictions—create a perspective, a vantage point from which to organize our thinking. But models of the mind, like all metaphors, have their limits and ultimately break down, particularly when they are over-used or treated as gospel, at which point they impede our ability to think.

There are a few specific points regarding the writing process itself to which I would like to turn. I try to use as few technical terms as possible, for they obscure, rather than express. I also try to avoid clichés of all sorts, including overused analytic words and phrases, for they drain life from "the story."

I find that phrases such as "in my opinion" and "I believe" must be closely associated with clinical material presented in the paper or with an established body of work (such as that of the French Psychosomatic School or Bowlby's work). When such backing is offered in some detail, the "opinion" or "belief" is no longer simply an opinion or belief.

Finally, because it seems to me that what is therapeutic about the psychoanalytic experience is more a matter of process than of content, I find that the language I use to describe what I am experiencing does best when it, too, is more verb than noun, more adverb than adjective, more active voice than passive voice.

Lest I leave the reader the impression that writing an analytic paper or book is only a sheer cliff to be climbed, it is important to say that the genre of the analytic essay is a literary art form. As such, it carries with it all the possibility of fulfillment in self-expression: the delight to be had in experiencing one's creativity; the satisfaction of making something distinctively one's own; and the feeling that one is contributing to a body of thought that one values. I experience great pleasure in writing—much of the time. I sometimes ask myself on bright spring mornings whether sitting at my desk writing is really the thing I most want to be doing, and usually the answer is yes ... but there are times when I feel that being a writer is a curse for which there is no escape or cure, except to sit down and write once more.

Index

Abram, J. 34
aliveness: emergence of 53,
    130–132; loss of 5; physical
    129–132; psychic 129, 130, 132;
    and transitional phenomena
    130; per Winnicott 53, 130–132
alpha elements 19, 133
alpha function 19
analytic field 59
analytic practice 103–114
analytic setting 18, 58, 84, 87, 89,
    142, 143, 148, 150, 154
analytic style: developing 19;
    versus technique 19, 59, 114
analytic theory: epistemological
    and ontological 9–32, as
    metaphor 98–103; of mind xiv,
    xv, 117–140
analytic third 59, 102, 114
analytic writing: description versus
    explanation 164; experience of
    xv: form of fiction 163–165; use
    of language 163–165
anxiety: from death instinct 123,
    125; expressed in play 11; fear of
    annihilation 122–123; leading
    edge of 12–13; persecutory
    and depressive 20–21; from

phantasized internal objects 21;
    phantasying, a solution to 124;
    primary cause of 122; from
    sexual instinct 122
autistic-contiguous position
    99–100
autistic psychopathology 41
autistic rocking: Tustin 37;
    Winnicott 37–38
autistic shape 38

Balint, M. 10
becoming destroyed 80–85,
    88, 95
becoming real 80–85, 95, 96
Beebe, B. 82
being: alive 16, 17, 54, 55, 130,
    135, 136, 138; destroyed
    80–83, 85, 86, 89, 92–93, 96;
    going-on- 16, 19, 36, 41, 130,
    131; state of 12, 14–18, 20–22,
    33, 35–37, 39–41, 43–44,
    51–53, 130–132
being and becoming: xiv, xv, 1–8,
    10, 13, 15, 19, 21, 136–138, 163
Berman, E. 10
beta elements 19, 133, 164
Binswanger, L. 15

167